Commitment

Commitment

The Dynamic of Strategy

Pankaj Ghemawat

THE FREE PRESS
A Division of Macmillan, Inc.
NEW YORK
Maxwell Macmillan Canada
TORONTO
Maxwell Macmillan International
NEW YORK OXFORD SINGAPORE SYDNEY

The Free Press
A Division of Macmillan, Inc.
866 Third Avenue, New York, N.Y. 10022

Maxwell Macmillan Canada, Inc.
1200 Eglinton Avenue East
Suite 200
Don Mills, Ontario M3C 3N1

Macmillan, Inc. is part of the Maxwell Communication Group of Companies.

Printed in the United States of America

printing number
1 2 3 4 5 6 7 8 9 10

Grateful acknowledgment is made for permission to reprint the following material:

Chapter 2: Excerpt from "The Love Song of J. Alfred Prufrock" in *Collected Poems 1909–1962* by T. S. Eliot, copyright 1936 by Harcourt Brace Jovanovich, Inc., copyright © 1964, 1963 by T. S. Eliot; reprinted by permission of Harcourt Brace Jovanovich, Inc., and Faber and Faber Ltd.

Chapter 6: Diagram from "Venture Capital in Transition" by Howard H. Stevenson, Daniel F. Muzyka and Jeffrey A. Timmons, *Journal of Business Venturing*, Vol. 2, pp. 103–121, copyright 1987 by Elsevier Science Publishing Co., Inc.; reprinted by permission of the publisher.

Chapter 7: Diagram from "Competitive Bidding in High-Risk Situations" by E. C. Capen, R. V. Clapp and W. M. Campbell, *Journal of Petroleum Technology*, Vol. 23, pp. 641–653, copyright 1971, Society of Petroleum Engineers; reprinted by permission of the copyright holder.

Chapter 7: Diagram from *Decision Making at the Top: The Shaping of Strategic Direction* by Gordon Donaldson and Jay W. Lorsch, copyright © 1983 by Basic Books, Inc.; reprinted by permission of Basic Books, Inc., Publishers, New York.

Library of Congress Cataloging-in-Publication Data

Ghemawat, Pankaj.
Commitment: the dynamic of strategy/Pankaj Ghemawat.
p. cm.
Includes bibliographical references (p.) and index.
ISBN 0–02–911575–2
1. Competition. 2. Organizational effectiveness. 3. Strategic planning. 4. Decision-making. 5. Managerial Economics. I. Title.
HD41.G48 1991
658.4'012—dc20 91–6527
CIP

TO

Richard E. Caves
Michael E. Porter

AND

A. Michael Spence

Contents

Preface

This book argues that managers must change the way they have traditionally thought about strategy. There are three points to the argument. First, managers have tended to think of strategy as a search for timeless bases of success. They should bring time back into the picture by recognizing that earlier choices constrain later ones; this is the dynamic I refer to as *commitment*. Second, managers have concentrated on choosing strategic principles to which individual choices are supposed to be subordinated. They should allot more attention to the few choices that individually embody significant commitment. Third, the strategic analyses managers do undertake have focused on long-run competitive positions. They also need to address the sustainability of such positions and the flexibility they afford in dealing with future uncertainties. The first point underpins the second and third ones because the cost of changing one's mind that is implicit in the concept of commitment is the only possible reason to think things through in depth.

Our systematic understanding of the consequences of commitment for business decision making is largely based on research into business economics. Industrial economists have demonstrated that costly-to-reverse commitments to durable, specialized factors are necessary for sustained differences in the performance of competing organizations, and have explored the conditions under which they are sufficient as well. Institutional economists have explained the structure of organizational coalitions (who gets what) in terms of the durability and specialization of the factors committed to them by various stakeholders. And informational economists have characterized the opportunity costs of commitment under conditions of uncertainty. Economics supplies the foundation of this book, although contributions from other disciplines are referred to as appropriate. The research that is relevant turns out to be of rather recent vintage: three-quarters of this book's references are to works that have been published (or written) since 1980; one-half date since 1985.

While this book is based on solid research, it is directed at the real world. Real managers cannot afford in-depth consideration of all the choices that are the individual links in the chain of commitment as they come up. This book will help managers identify the (few) choices that do deserve to be analyzed in depth, and will present a framework for analysis that improves on the ones they currently use. In order to make the book readable without sacrificing its rigor, I have kept it short, highlighted the key conceptual propositions as sentence headings, illustrated the concepts with detailed examples, and (mostly) limited references to the number necessary to make it clear that the argument is based on more than sheer assertion.

I began to think of writing a book of this sort in 1983, when I started to teach an elective course on strategy. As a graduate student at Harvard in the late 1970s, I had already been exposed to the commitment-centered "new" industrial economics. I spent 1982–1983 as a management consultant with McKinsey and Company and came away with the sense that a potentially large payoff could be had by operationalizing the concept of commitment. The years I have since spent at the Harvard Business School have been devoted, directly and indirectly, to doing so.

Although many people have helped me through this multiyear effort, I cannot but begin by citing my three thesis advisors at Harvard, Richard Caves, Michael Porter and Michael Spence. They sparked my interest in the power of scholarly thinking to illumine business strategy, steered the scholarly component of that interest toward industrial economics, and continued to shape it as teachers, collaborators and role models. Caves and Porter have endured, in addition, several earlier drafts of this manuscript. This book is dedicated to them in appreciation for their kindness and their inspiration.

Many other colleagues, most of whom also have a special interest in business strategy, have commented perceptively on parts or all of this manuscript. I am especially grateful to Carliss Baldwin,

Joseph Bower, Stephen Bradley, David Collis, Herman Daems, Richard Hackman, Rebecca Henderson, Marvin Lieberman, Jay Lorsch, Anita McGahan, Drazen Prelec, Elizabeth Teisberg and David Yoffie for their advice. Of course, none of these advisors should automatically be assumed to agree with the opinions I express.

I must also thank my MBA students in the Industry and Competitive Analysis course at the Harvard Business School for their enthusiasm in working with and clarifying the ideas in this book, and the School itself for its unwavering support. I have promised my wife, Anuradha, that I will not write another book (at least not right away); if I do, though, it will be dedicated to her for the ways in which she, more than any one else, helped me with this one.

Cambridge, Mass.
January 1991

1

→⟫ ⟪←

Strategy: The Failure of Success Factors

If we wish to increase the yield of grain in a certain field and on analysis it appears that the soil lacks potash, potash may be said to be the strategic (or limiting) factor.

—Chester I. Barnard, *The Functions of the Executive*

Something has gone wrong with using strategy as a guide to managerial action. Indexes of business periodicals suggest that while the concept of strategy gained share in the market for business ideas in the 1970s, it lost market share in the 1980s. This decline does *not* reflect a perception that the problem of strategy has practically been solved. Rather, the perception that seems to have developed is that while strategy is easy to formulate, it is awfully hard to implement. As a result, an increasing fraction of what does get written about strategy calls, in effect, for abandoning the concept. Those who might oppose such calls seem to be preoccupied, instead, with arguing the superiority of their particular strategic doctrine over all others. What went wrong? History suggests a concise answer to that question.

STRATEGY HAS COME TO FOCUS ON SUCCESS FACTORS.

Chester Barnard (1938) introduced strategy to business with his discussion of strategic factors; the epigraph to this chapter is a sample.[1] Barnard recognized the managerial impossibility of apprehending and acting all at once on the many factors that impinge on organizational performance. He therefore suggested focusing on and changing one factor at a time. This strategic factor was supposed to be selected so as to capitalize on complementarities: so as to allow a favorable change in the total situation *via* a change in one of its parts.

The example of potash, which most of us never have to worry about, should hint at the situationality of the original conception of the strategic factor. But Barnard (1938, p. 204) went even farther than that:

> When the need [for potash] has been determined, a new situation has arisen because of the fact of knowledge or assumption that potash is the limiting factor; and instead of potash, the limiting factor *obtaining potash* then becomes the strategic factor; and this will change progressively into *obtaining* the money to *buy* potash, then *finding* John to go after potash, then *getting* machines and men to *spread* potash, etc., etc. Thus the determination of the strategic factor is itself the decision which at once reduces purpose to a new level, compelling search for a new strategic factor in the new situation.

In other words, the strategic factor was originally conceived of as a will-o'-the-wisp.

This conception proved, predictably, to be impractically intricate. As a result, the field of strategy lay dormant for a while. It was not until the 1950s or 1960s (depending on whose claims to priority one credits) that refinements to Barnard's concept began to be proposed. While the refinements were various, they all implied the usefulness of more stable bases for strategic abstraction than Barnard's short-lived successive constraints. The most alluring expedient was to hunt for stable bases of success, for *success factors*. The search for success factors is what the enterprise of strategy has largely been about ever since.

The last statement will be controversial. One way to corroborate it would be to classify beliefs about strategy and explain why the prescriptions of each "school" do in fact rest on success factors.

Such surveys of the field of strategy seem, however, to be in excess supply rather than in excess demand.[2] I will therefore use a specific case to illustrate the reliance of managers and would-be managers on success factors.

The case concerns Wal-Mart Stores' discount retailing business.[3] In the 1970s and 1980s, that business grew at an annual rate of 40%, generated an annual return on equity (ROE) of 35%, and made the company's founder, Mr. Sam Walton, the richest person and one of the most celebrated managers in the United States. By 1990, Wal-Mart was on the verge of surpassing both Sears, Roebuck and K Mart to become the largest general-merchandise retailer in the United States. I chose to write a case about this situation because it was evidently ripe for strategic deconstruction. The strategic lessons drawn from the Wal-Mart case play across a spectrum of success factors, some of which are elaborated on below.

Market Power

An unusually high proportion of Wal-Mart's stores were located in small towns where there was no local competition from other discounters. So although its operating expenses were 8% lower than the average for other discounters (partly because of its rural focus), it priced only 5% below them. In other words, market power allowed Wal-Mart to hang on to some of its cost advantage as a discounter instead of being forced to pass all the savings on to its customers.

Time-based Competition

Wal-Mart had developed the capability of responding exceptionally quickly to changes in consumer buying patterns. Private communications links let it obtain feedback from its stores within 90 minutes of the time they closed and alter the mix of products being shipped to its stores at least once each day, if not more often. Wal-Mart also managed to replenish the stock in its stores twice a week on average, compared to once every two weeks for Sears, Roebuck and K Mart.

Organization

Wal-Mart's organization seemed attuned to the distinctive requirements of running a multisite service operation. Although most operating decisions at Wal-Mart were unusually decentralized (down to the store level), top management received unusually detailed numbers on operating performance and paid an unusual amount of attention to them. In addition, all top managers spent three or four days a week in the field visiting Wal-Mart stores to get a sense of developments that might not be evident from the numbers. To cap things off, there had historically been little separation of ownership and management at the top of the pyramid. Wal-Mart had been run actively by Sam Walton, its founder and principal shareholder, until he retired as chief executive officer in 1988.

Total Customer Satisfaction

Wal-Mart is often said to have practiced total customer satisfaction. Its most profitable stores were the ones that offered customers the broadest and best mix of merchandise of any store in the area, and at consistently lower prices, too. And even when Wal-Mart faced competitors that carried much the same merchandise at comparable prices in look-alike stores (e.g., K Mart), it managed to secure higher consumer ratings. Wal-Mart's logo, its greeters and other little touches had all been cited in this context, leading us to the next story about its success.

Learning

David Glass, who succeeded Sam Walton as chief executive officer in 1988, described discount retailing as a business of details, one in which there were many ways for Wal-Mart to lose the three extra percentage points of operating margin it earned in the mid-1980s. Wal-Mart had clearly gone to great lengths to learn how best to handle details. According to one inspired analyst's report, loading trucks to minimize store space devoted to the back room, unpacking boxes, scheduling part-time labor, displaying jeans to promote tie-in sales of hats, juggling fixture heights for maximum impact and hundreds of other activities had all been analyzed (not just answered) by the company over the years.

Empowerment

Discount retailing is a labor-intensive business in which shop floor workers play a critical role in overall operating efficiency. But they are also a major cost element: payroll expenses account for about 40% of the value added in this business. Such considerations place a premium on trying to motivate workers by empowering them, instead of simply paying them more. There were several indications that Wal-Mart had compiled an exceptional record in this regard. For instance, it had been voted one of the hundred best companies to work for in the United States, in spite of its relatively tight-fisted pay scale.

Leadership

As founder, controlling owner, hands-on manager and cheerleader, Sam Walton had played an atypically important role at Wal-Mart. Many Wal-Mart watchers tended to see the company as the shadow of the man at the top. In their eyes, Walton was the company's real success factor because of the leadership he offered in areas such as frugality, customer-sensitivity, and enthusiasm. "Hard" evidence of Walton's contribution included the grisly observation that the price of Wal-Mart stock had slumped when it was first announced that he had leukemia.

This list has covered only a few fashionable success factors, not all the ones that are proposed in the case of Wal-Mart. My sense, however, is that while additional success factors such as configuration, location, market share and strategic intent could be retrofitted to the Wal-Mart story, the exercise would be tedious, rather than necessary. The managerial tendency to abstract about strategy in terms of success factors should already be clear.

Success factors are a shaky foundation for strategy.

Success factors have their uses, some of which will be discussed later in this book. It would not be sensible, however, to base the entire edifice of strategy on them, for four reasons. First, it is usually hard to identify the success factors relevant to a particular situation. Second, even when a success factor has been diagnosed to be relevant, the implications for the levers managers must pull are not completely concrete. Third, the success factor approach lacks generality because it implicitly assumes that success factors are undervalued. Finally, in view of its other defects, it would be reassuring if the success factor approach to strategy contained some self-justification: a reason why strategic thinking is necessary in the first place. It does not. The rest of this section elaborates on these four defects.

Lack of Identification

The generic success factors flagged in the previous section range across the imaginable spectrum, from the bright economic lights of market power, in which no human beings are visible, to the shadowier tones of empowerment and leadership, in which humans are all. Their diversity reflects the fact that strategists currently worship at many separate churches. It is sometimes asserted that such diversity isn't a bad thing. Managers cannot, however, be so ecumenical. Having to track the full complement of success factors flagged in the case of Wal-Mart would virtually be equivalent to having to track everything. This could only be construed as a repudiation of the search for managerially useful abstractions inaugurated by Chester Barnard.

Nor does contingency theory, with its emphasis on the uniqueness of each situation, promise much relief. A contingent perspective on success factors would imply that the ones to focus on depend on the specifics of the situation. This might seem useful in narrowing the number of success factors to be tracked in any specific situation. Unfortunately, agreement is frequently as elusive on specific success factors as on generic ones. The specifics of the Wal-Mart case, for instance, lend themselves to a host of interpretations, each purporting to explain all by itself the company's ability to earn an operating margin of 7.7% on its 1984 revenues versus 4.8% for the average discount retailer. While several (if not all) of the success factors cited above can be dressed up into "complete" explanations of Wal-Mart's above-average profitability, boredom-through-repetition will be minimized by considering a fresh one: *configurational efficiency*.

Wal-Mart's configuration differed from other discounters' in two respects: an unusually high proportion of its in-bound merchandise moved to its stores via its distribution centers instead of directly, and its regional vice presidents operated out of corporate headquarters instead of offices in the field. According to the company's own calculations, this configuration created efficiencies on the order of 3% to 4% of revenues. Thus Wal-Mart's superior profitability might entirely be attributed to the efficiency of its configuration. Yet surely there was more to its success than the architecture of its system.

The embarrassing abundance of candidate success factors and

the consequent difficulty of figuring out which one(s) to focus on reflect more than just the juiciness of the Wal-Mart story. Both conditions tend to be chronic, for the following reason. Barnard's notion of the strategic factor was conceived around factor complementarities, around the whole being more than the sum of its parts. This conception has been retained in the subsequent search for success factors. But it is well known, at least to economists and accountants, that the sum of the marginal products of complementary factors will exceed their total product. In other words, complementarities imply that it will be easy to propose success factors that promise a big bang per increment of managerial effort, and correspondingly hard to figure out which one(s) to focus on. Since strategy does demand such a focus, this compromises the usefulness of the success factor approach.

Lack of Concreteness

Even if the relevant success factor(s) can be identified, that does not quite solve the managerial problem of what to do about it. The problem is that the mechanism that is supposed to mediate between the organization's stock of success factors and its performance is black-boxed, in the sense that the causal processes that make it work in concrete situations are not spelled out. More precisely, the success factor approach rests not only on abstract objects (which have been deemed necessary to strategy) but also on hermetic laws about their effects.

This lack of concreteness and the complications it creates are clearest in the case of "soft" success factors. Consider, for instance, the success factor of leadership. The inference that leadership is important does not tell managers how to improve their leadership quotient. Rather, the diversity of organizational situations ensures the diversity of the levers that managers must actually pull to become more effective leaders.

This problem is not peculiar to soft success factors. At the other end of the spectrum, even the "hard" success factor of market power is no more than a conceptual filing cabinet (albeit an exceptionally useful one) whose specific contents vary from situation to situation. What a manager must do to help the organization accumulate market power is necessarily specialized to the situation at hand.

Once again, the problem runs deeper than may be apparent at first glance. One of the major themes of the philosophy of science in the 1980s was that attempts to explain *any* phenomenon in terms of abstract objects (e.g., organizational performance in terms of success factors) require specificity about the causal processes that actually connect the abstract objects and real, observable variables.[4] By implication, overarching laws can be uncovered only if high-level causal processes can be found. But the content of the success factor approach, such as it is, appears to rest on many low-level causal processes rather than on a few high-level ones. That is why success factors seem to be simulacra rather than *real keys* to organizational performance.

Lack of Generality

Success factor fans inclined to dismiss the two problems discussed above as being too abstract to worry about must contend with a third, more pressing one. Strategic theories that trade on success factors prescribe augmentation of the organization's stock of the relevant one(s). The underlying presumption is that the cost-benefit ratio of such augmentation is less than one: that the marginal product of the success factor exceeds its marginal cost. This is an arbitrary assumption that restricts the generality of such theories.

An illustration may, once again, help clarify the argument. Many statistical studies have uncovered positive associations between the market shares of businesses and their profitability. The implied theory of market share as *the* success factor has been widely diffused; large, well-funded corporations interlocked in both oligopolistic competition and membership in the Profit Impact of Market Strategy (PIMS) program seem particularly attuned to this message. What would happen if the significant competitors in concentrated industries all tried to increase their respective market shares? Given the constraint that the sum of their market shares cannot exceed 100%, one suspects that that would lead to collective impairment of their performance. It is in this rather troubling sense that theories that trade on undervalued success factors may be suspect rather than merely arbitrary in their parametric assumptions.

Similar limitations apply to the other success factors that I have listed. While it may be nice to have market power, why doesn't competition to acquire it dissipate the profits expected of it? While faster may be better than slower, won't accelerating competition eventually eliminate the gains from further speeding up activities? To ask the same questions another way, why can't Sears, Roebuck, which has studied Wal-Mart and tried to become more like it, seem to close the competitive gap? Saying that Wal-Mart capitalizes on the key success factor(s) in the retailing environment and that Sears doesn't is not very satisfactory for the reason best expressed by the game theorists von Neumann and Morgenstern (1944): it is hard to be satisfied with the generality of prescriptions whose success depends on their not being widely grasped.

There *is* a more satisfying explanation for the persistent asymmetry between Wal-Mart and Sears, but it doesn't come from the success factor approach. It derives, instead, from the dynamic mentioned in the next subsection and elaborated in the next chapter.

Lack of Necessity

In view of the other defects of success factors, it would be useful if strategic theories that traded on them contained a self-justification, a reason why more-or-less elaborate theories are necessary in the first place. Otherwise, one might be tempted to dispense with strategy in order to get on with things. The success factor approach does nothing to curb that temptation. It suggests no rationale for trying to grasp reality through the idealization of a success factor or two instead of groping at it through trial and error.

The success factor approach fails in this regard, as it did in the previous one, because it does not give history its due. It does not adequately account for the constraints imposed both by past decisions on current ones, and by current ones on those yet to come. Ignoring dynamic constraints undermines the case for ever taking a deep look into the future, for thinking strategically as opposed to myopically. The reason is that in the assumed absence of dynamic constraints, myopic policies will afford as much value as far-sighted ones, and greater ease of operation.

To summarize this section, it is hard to identify strategic success factors and make their effects concrete, and treacherous to count on their being undervalued. To make matters worse, the success factor approach doesn't really explain the necessity of thinking non-myopically in the first place. Strategy cannot, as a result, be reduced to a matter of identifying and chasing success factors.

The Failure of Success Factors Isn't Fatal to the Enterprise of Strategy.

This is not the first time that the defects of the success factor approach have been discovered. Previous discoveries have tended, however, to climax in a denial of the value of trying to think through things ahead of time, i.e., nonmyopically. That denial isn't helpful to managers looking to strategy to help improve the quality of the choices that they must make. Nor does it ring true. I will use the Wal-Mart example, once again, to illustrate the two most popular forms of denial and the problems with them.

Predetermination

One popular way of denying that strategic thinking can make a difference is to assert that choices are, for practical purposes, predetermined. For instance, the "population ecology" school of strategy postulates that organizational form does not fall within the realm of conscious choice and that once it is set, it largely determines the organization's subsequent course of action.[5] In other words, it supposes that an organization's strategy is predetermined at its "birth."

Since Wal-Mart is a retailer, the most obvious rationalization of its success in these terms is the one suggested by the theory of the retailing cycle. According to this theory, retailing formats succeed one another and as this goes on, the operators of old formats have trouble adjusting to competition from new ones. So the theory of the retailing cycle is basically a theory of predetermination by initial format. It would explain Wal-Mart's success in terms of its early emphasis on a new format, the small-town discount store, that ultimately proved to be successful.

A closer look at Wal-Mart's early history tends, however, to contradict rather than corroborate predetermination in the spirit of the retailing cycle. Wal-Mart's precursor, run by Sam Walton, was a chain of five-and-dimes in rural Arkansas that had become the most successful franchisee of Ben Franklin stores in the country. The theory of the retailing cycle would not lead one to expect that this organization would have tried to transform itself into a discount store format, much less succeeded. Yet that is what happened.

Wal-Mart wasn't the only dime store to make itself over into a successful discount retailer: K Mart (previously S. S. Kresge) did too. More broadly, common sense suggests that managers do make important, apparently discretionary choices: that organizational change is more than just the undirected mutation envisioned by population ecologists. This book assumes as much and focuses on improving the quality of such choices.

Luck

A second popular way of denying that strategic thinking can make a difference is to assert that luck is all, that *ex ante* uncertainty is the only reason for *ex post* differences in the performance of organizations. Explanations of success and failure in terms of purely random processes have long been popular in economics and have recently begun to infiltrate the literature on strategy.[6]

Wal-Mart's success might be rationalized as good luck in three respects. Wal-Mart may have been lucky that its idea of operating large, almost oversized stores in small towns worked out: it was not clear, ahead of time, that towns with fewer than 100,000 people could support discount stores. It may have also been lucky in that the region it focused on, the Sunbelt, grew relatively quickly in the 1970s and early 1980s. And it may have been lucky again in that its potential competitors, national discounters and regional five-and-dime franchises, were slow to imitate its pattern of locating discount stores in small towns even after that pattern had been sanctified by success.

To argue, however, that Wal-Mart's success is *entirely* a matter of luck is to strain credibility. Very many strokes of luck, rather than just one, would be needed to explain the consistently rapid appreciation of Wal-Mart's stock. Since consistent luck is rather far-fetched, that would seem to argue against a purely random explanation of Wal-Mart's success.

More systematic analysis supports the presumption that flows from the Wal-Mart case: that luck is far from all.[7] This is useful because if luck overshadowed everything else, the connection between predictions and outcomes would be too loose for thinking ahead to be of help. This book assumes that managers have *some* ability to predict the future.

Summary

Strategy has focused, for the most part, on success factors. Theories of strategy that trade on success factors prescribe algorithms, usually single-factor ones, for improving performance. But the whole idea of identifying a success factor and then chasing it seems to have something in common with the ill-considered medieval hunt for the *philosopher's stone,* a substance that would transmute everything it touched into gold.

The failure of the success factor approach has led some to abandon the quest for managerially useful abstractions that motivated the field of strategy. This book takes a more constructive tack. It bears down on observations of dynamic constraints to identify a stable strategic factor that is something more than Barnard's notion of a fleeting strategic factor but less than a stable success factor, *commitment*. Commitment is to be thought of as the cause of strategic persistence. It is a constraint that must be reckoned with, not a recipe for success. The next chapter elaborates on this definition and shows that commitment is a superior basis for thinking about strategy because it escapes the problems endemic to success factors. The chapters that follow operationalize the concept of commitment.

2

→⟫ ⟪←

Commitment: The Persistence of Strategies

> At every moment of my life there open before me divers possibilities: I can do this or that. If I do this, I shall be A the moment after; if I do that, I shall be B . . . Man must not only make himself: the weightiest thing he has to do is to determine *what* he is going to be.
>
> —José Ortega y Gasset, *History as a System*

> In a minute there is time
> For decisions and revisions which a minute will reverse.
>
> —T. S. Eliot, "The Love Song of J. Alfred Prufrock"

The previous chapter suggested that it would be useful to find a way of thinking about strategy that is more ambitious than Chester Barnard's shifting strategic factor, but less ambitious than a success factor. One intermediate option is to substitute the notion of *cumulative* constraint for Barnard's *successive* constraints, to postulate that organizations tend to persist with their respective strategies over time. I define *commitment* as the tendency toward such persistence. The remainder of this book focuses on commitment as the basis for thinking about strategy.

In this particular chapter, I elaborate on the concept of commitment and show that it escapes all four of the problems endemic to success factors. Commitment is identified as *the* strategic (i.e., limiting or constraining) factor by the generally agreed evidence on how strategies evolve over time. The concept of commitment gains concreteness from the high-level causal processes that it rests on, processes that involve lock-in, lock-out, lags and inertia. Commitment underlies the only general explanation for persistent differences in the performance of organizations. Finally, the irreversibility implicit in commitment makes it important to look deep into the future instead of behaving myopically.

I DEFINE COMMITMENT AS THE TENDENCY OF STRATEGIES TO PERSIST OVER TIME.

People commonly conceive of commitment as a good thing. That much is clear from the uses to which the word is put in commercial speech. Consider, as an example, the issue of *BusinessWeek* that I had at hand when I wrote this. There were 11 advertisements in that issue that contained the words "commitment" and "committed." Because their usage was similar, I will cite just three representative examples. Upjohn declared its commitment to improving the quality of life to be greater than ever. Siemens said that it was fulfilling its commitment to keep its customers and employees working smarter, not just harder. And American Airlines announced that it was committed to mechanical excellence.

In a strategic context, this usage of commitment would send us back to chapter 1: commitment would be just another success factor and therefore subject to all the associated problems. Avoidance of those problems is my reason for defining commitment differently, in descriptive terms, as the tendency of organizations to persist with their broad courses of action or strategies. Under the terms of this definition, commitment should be thought of as a dynamic constraint on strategy, one that is cumulative instead of successive in the sense of Barnard. Note that such a constraint is neither intrinsically good nor bad. Both Wal-Mart and Sears, Roebuck persisted with their respective strategies in retailing through most of the 1970s and 1980s, but with very different results.

The concept of commitment can be elucidated by comparing the two very different depictions of choice in the epigraphs to this chapter. What differences in perspective account for the difference between Ortega's picture, in which choice is all, and Eliot's Prufrock, who pictures choice as nothing at all? The essential difference is that the former, unlike the latter, presumes that initial choice constrains subsequent behavior. The clearest way to grasp the nature of the constraint emphasized by Ortega is to note that the choice he depicts matters only to the extent that it is difficult to flip-flop from A to B or vice versa. In contrast, the trivial view that Eliot's Prufrock takes of choice is based on the assumption that such flip-flops are easy. I define commitment as the degree of difficulty of flip-flops. More precisely, a strategy embodies commitment to the extent that, if adopted, it is likely to persist.

The difficulty of strategic flip-flops can be formalized in the terms proposed by Ortega. Suppose that A and B are the only two strategies available to the organization, and that the evolution of its choice between the two is given by the probability matrix in Exhibit 2.1, which is perfectly general as bimatrixes go. In the context of this binary setup, to hypothesize commitment is to suggest that the organization is more likely to be engaged in strategy A in the future if A (rather than B) is the one that it engages in initially. The difference between these likelihoods will depend on the time frame (*t*) being contemplated. The organization's initial strategy is unlikely to have much of an effect on its strategy a century later. But today's strategy is unlikely, for the typical organization observed on a typical day, to have changed by tomorrow. The next section tests commitment, thus conceived, for descriptive content.

Exhibit 2.1 The Strategic Probability Matrix

		STRATEGY AT TIME t	
		A	B
STRATEGY AT TIME 0	A	p	1 – p
	B	1 – q	q

DYNAMIC	CONDITION
COMMITMENT	$p > 1 - q$
MEMORYLESSNESS	$p = 1 - q$
CONTRADICTION	$p < 1 - q$

COMMITMENT IS CRUCIAL TO EXPLAINING STRATEGIC DYNAMICS.

Is commitment really characteristic, over time, of the strategies that organizations pursue? And if so, to what degree? In order to answer these questions, I should be more explicit about what I mean by "strategy." Strategy is one of those sponge words so soaked with meaning that interpretations can be squeezed out of it by the bucketful. The perspectives on strategy discussed in the last chapter should have hinted at the diversity of the interpretations that are possible. In developing a general theory of strategy, it is useful to start with a definition, necessarily spare, of the content of strategy that is acceptable all around.

The one aspect of strategy that is widely accepted is that it manifests itself in broad patterns of behavior. The consensus is useful because it connects strategy to specific observable variables. Danny Miller, Peter Friesen, Henry Mintzberg and others at McGill University exploited this connection to trace organizational behavior over periods spanning several decades. They isolated streams of organizational actions in selected areas, interpreted patterns in these streams in terms of mutually exclusive courses of action (*strategies*) and inferred periods in organizational history by considering broad continuity and change in the pursuit of various strategies. They found that strategic continuity was the norm, but that it was punctuated by brief periods of radical change (see Exhibit 2.2). Based on Miller and Friesen's (1984) scoring rules, the average time between changes of strategy by the organizations in their sample equaled six years.

Commitment seems to be the only logical explanation for punctuated equilibria of the sort depicted in Exhibit 2.2, for two reasons.[1] These are best articulated in terms of the bimatrix setup discussed earlier, within which commitment implied that p was greater than $1 - q$. First, probabilistic calculations show that the inequality implied by commitment makes strategic continuity more likely than strategic

Exhibit 2.2 The Dynamic of Strategy

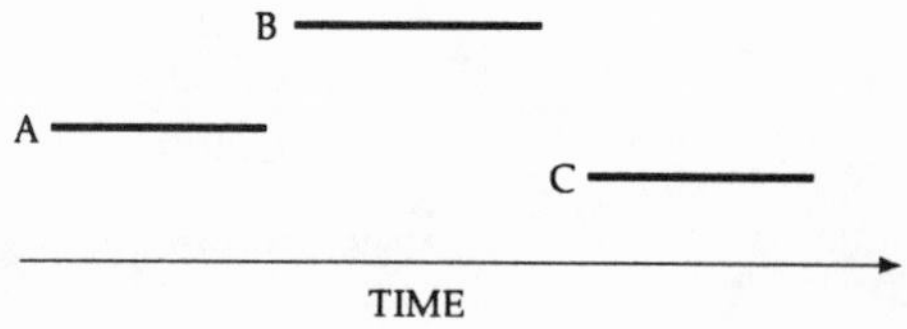

B

A

C

TIME

Exh. 2-2

transitions: continuity is the norm, although flip-flops supply punctuation.[2]

Second, commitment seems necessary as well as sufficient to explain the punctuation of strategies apparent in patterns of organizational behavior. Note that the two alternatives to commitment are that the probability p is equal to or less than the probability $1 - q$. If the two probabilities were equal, the organization's strategy after the passage of time t would be entirely independent of its initial strategy. And if p were less than $1 - q$, that would imply an even higher frequency of strategic change than if the two probabilities were equal. The dynamic depicted in Exhibit 2.2 contradicts both these alternatives. There is no easy explanation for punctuated equilibria unless history matters in the way implied by commitment.

Commitment is caused by lock-in, lock-out, lags and inertia.

Chapter 1 explained why theories of strategy that trade on success factors suffer from a lack of concreteness. Commitment suggests a more concrete theory of strategy because the processes that cause strategic persistence can be specified at a (relatively) high level. Four high-level processes are involved: lock-in, lock-out, lags and inertia. The rest of this section elaborates on each of these possible causes of commitment.

Lock-In

One reason an organization might persist with its initial strategy over time is that it may have been locked into that strategy by its actions in the interim. The case of the Boeing 747 will illustrate this cause of commitment. By the time it had spent well over a billion dollars to develop the 747's wide-bodied airframe, Boeing had reason to be committed to a "747 strategy," to persist with its efforts to assemble and sell the plane. At that point in the program, the net investment in the 747 considerably exceeded the company's net worth. Most of the costs were accounted for by factors such as know-how and production capacity whose value was predicated on continued pursuit of the 747 strategy. As a result, Boeing was sunk unless it could make the 747 fly.

The example of the 747 indicates that investment in certain kinds of factors can lead to commitment via lock-in. It also exposes the attributes that factors must have if investment in them is to have this effect. First and most broadly, factors must be *durable* if they are to wield any historical influence. Second, they must be *specialized* or else they would be equally appropriate to all strategies. Finally, durability and specialization, while necessary conditions, are insufficient. The factors involved must also be *untradeable* on well-functioning markets: if they weren't, there would be no presumption in favor of keeping as opposed to selling them and, therefore, no economic reason to persist with the strategy they had originally been intended to underpin. It will be convenient to refer to durable, specialized, untradeable factors as *sticky*. To adopt some terminology recently proposed by Porter (1990, p. 77), basic factors such as natural resources, unskilled labor and debt capital are unlikely to be as sticky as more advanced factors.

Of the three conditions required for factor stickiness, durability and specialization are relatively transparent. The condition of untradeability, however, warrants further comment. There are several (overlapping) reasons why particular factors might not easily be tradeable: recontracting costs, buyer and supplier power, imperfect information and complementarities with other, untradeable factors. In the case of the 747, untradeability stemmed from the fact that the two competitors that might have otherwise been buyers, Lockheed and McDonnell Douglas, had quickly committed themselves to a smaller, rather different wide-body design.

The theory of market failures predicts, and the evidence tends to confirm, that intangible factors (e.g., relationships and information) are typically less tradeable, and in that sense stickier, than tangible factors (e.g., plant, physical property and equipment). This serves as a reminder of the inadvisability of weighting factors by their toe-stubbing capacity. The reminder is useful because there does seem to be a tendency, attributable to perceptual biases, to give tangibles more and intangibles less than their respective due. For instance, the sticky factor stressed in journalistic accounts of Boeing's commitment, by the late 1960s, to the 747 was its (tangible) new manufacturing facility, probably because the world's largest enclosed space made good copy. It seems, however, that the intangible know-how required to jump from big single-aisle planes to jumbo wide-bodied ones was actually a bigger deal than the factory itself. For one thing, the know-how had cost Boeing more. For another, the expenditure on know-how had been concentrated in an earlier

Exhibit 2.3 Lock-In

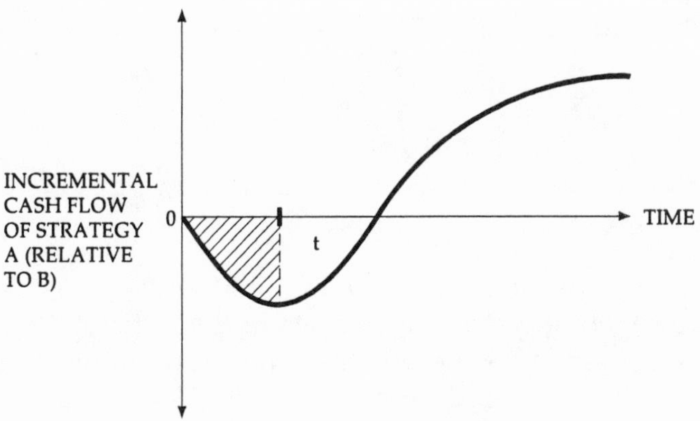

phase of the development cycle. One would not be too far off the mark in averring that it was the stickiness of intangible factors, rather than tangible ones, that had sown the seeds of commitment in this instance.

The ways the stickiness of both tangible and intangible factors can lead to commitment can be synthesized. Suppose that strategy A involves the accumulation of sticky factors and strategy B, the "base case," does not. Exhibit 2.3 schematizes the implications of pursuing strategy A instead of strategy B. If the organization initially engages in strategy A, it can, in comparing the two strategies at time *t*, ignore the crosshatched area in the exhibit as long as that area is accounted for by investments in factors whose value is limited to the organization's continued pursuit of strategy A. In that eventuality, persistence with the initial strategy will be favored even in the face of some bad news about it. Thus Boeing was committed to the 747 strategy once it was far enough along the development cycle, even though it might not have initiated development had it fully anticipated the difficulties that lay ahead, particularly the increases in take-off weight that would be demanded by its launch customer, Pan American (Newhouse 1982).

Lock-Out

Lock-out, as a cause of commitment, is the mirror image of lock-in. Consider, as an example, Reynolds Metals' decision to shut down its alumina refinery at Hurricane Creek, Arkansas, after sev-

Exhibit 2.4 Reynolds and Its Refinery

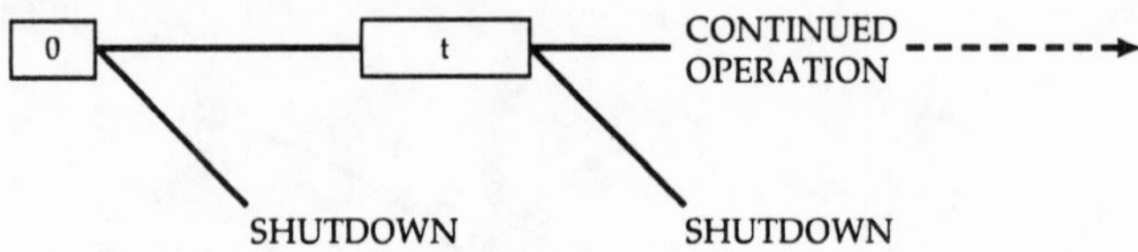

eral years of unprofitable operations. Shutdown locked Reynolds out of ever operating that refinery again. Even if aluminum prices did recover, it would be uneconomic to restart the 40-year-old, high-cost facility since it would need to be cleaned out, readjusted and "debottlenecked," a costly procedure that might take two years or longer to restore the original level of operating efficiency. The operating cost of the Hurricane Creek refinery had already been almost as high as the full cost of new, efficiently scaled facilities in Australia. The extra burden of restarting it would push its effective costs above theirs, ensuring that expansion in Australia would block exhumation in Arkansas. That is why Exhibit 2.4 rules out the shutdown→operation sequence: in shutting down the Hurricane Creek refinery, Reynolds was committing itself to keeping that facility shut.

Note that the shutdown strategy was bound to persist not because it involved investment in sticky factors, but because it entailed disinvestment (or failure to maintain previous investment) in refining capacity. This example shows that commitment's domain extends beyond factor-additive investment processes to encompass factor-subtractive (or nonadditive) disinvestment processes. The latter can create commitment because of the difficulty of recalling discarded opportunities on the original terms.

Economists are quite used to accounting for lock-out. As Samuelson's (1976, p. 475) introductory textbook puts it, "The economist . . . realizes that some of the most important costs attributable to doing one thing rather than another stem from the *forgone opportunities* that have to be sacrificed in doing this one thing." Managers, however, have been accused of being less than competent in this regard. Such is, for instance, the implication of Hayes and Garvin's (1982, p. 78) "Managing as if Tomorrow Mattered":

> One reason companies so often become trapped in this sort of disinvestment spiral—deferred investment leading to reduced profitability, which further reduces the incentive to invest—is

> that discounting techniques make the implicit assumption that investment processes are reversible. That is, if one sells an asset, one can always buy it back; or if one delays in investment, one can always make it at some later date with no penalty other than that implied by the company's discount rate. No company, however, can be sure of recovering lost ground quite so easily. To regain its position, a company may have to spend a good deal more than if it had made the investment when first proposed. As time passes, downward spirals become much more difficult to arrest.

Hayes and Garvin go on to argue that investment is an act of faith that cannot and should not be subordinated to economic analysis. That seems to me to be the wrong conclusion, for reasons expounded in the chapters that follow. They do deserve credit, however, for emphasizing that shifting into reverse or staying in neutral can compel just as much commitment as pressing forward with investment. Lock-out may be a less direct cause of commitment than lock-in, but it is no less important: opportunity costs are just as real as out-of-pocket costs.

Lock-out, like lock-in, looms largest as a source of dynamic constraint in relation to factors that are not traded on well-functioning markets (e.g., alumina refineries or airframe designs). The difference is that lock-in stems from the difficulty of disposing of sticky factors under such conditions, whereas lock-out reflects the subsequent difficulty of reacquiring and redeploying them. The second difficulty matters because it seems to be suboptimal for an organization pursuing a particular strategy to maintain reserves of all the sticky factors that might be necessary for the pursuit of alternatives. To the extent that significant costs must be incurred in reactivating dormant factors, reacquiring abandoned ones or, more generally, recreating lapsed opportunities to deploy particular factors in particular ways, the strategy selected initially will, because of the implied lock-out from the alternatives, tend to persist.

Lags

The obvious way to unify the two causes of commitment discussed above is to postulate that an organization's ability to act upon opportunities as they present themselves is constrained by the stocks of factors that it has accumulated. This perspective on the organization, with its emphasis on factor adjustment costs, is implicit in some of the earlier writing about strategy.[3] It also suggests a third cause of commitment: lags in adjusting the organization's stocks of sticky factors to desired levels.

For an example of such lags and how they can lead to commitment, consider Coors' national rollout in the late 1970s and early 1980s. It was clear from the outset that the switch from a regional to a national strategy would take a decade, or at least the better part of one. Coors would have to modify its traditional preoccupation with production, develop additional marketing know-how, build a national clientele by advertising more per barrel than entrenched competitors, establish relationships with distributors in 39 new states, open its first new manufacturing facility since 1873, and so forth. Irrespective of how one classifies Coors' strategy in the years in which it implemented these sweeping changes, it is clear that the rollout had a chance of working only if Coors stuck with it until it could test the key advantage alleged for the national strategy, economies of scale in advertising, on a national or near-national network. So when Coors rolled out, it committed itself to acting in a particular way for a substantial period of time.

Implicit in lags is the idea that crash programs can be costly: that accelerating adjustment may, beyond a certain threshold, require a more than proportionate increase in rates of expenditure on adjustment. There are at least three reasons why such acceleration can be costly. First, as attempts are made to use time ever more intensively, diminishing returns may set in. Second, acceleration may exacerbate the constraints of bounded rationality (which are elaborated in the next chapter). Third, acceleration may also be costly in the sense of reducing flexibility; this point is developed at greater length in chapter 6.

The literature on strategy has mostly been too impatient to give lags their due. Guesstimates of their average duration will help underscore their importance. As a rule of thumb, marketing variables, particularly those related to communications, are the only ones that can be changed significantly in less than one year (Bonoma 1981); even so, the sticky factor they are supposed to influence, customer base, tends to move much more slowly in many instances. Two to three years are required to build the average plant (Ghemawat 1987). Casual evidence suggests that building a new distribution system or altering an existing one may take even longer. The mean lag in returns from expenditures on research and development tends to be of the order of four to six years (Cohen and Levin 1989). It may take as long as seven years to implement major changes in human resource practices (Skinner 1981). Corporate restructuring may require a decade or longer because of the wrangling that tends to accompany major transfers of value (Donaldson 1989).

I should also add that it is possible, at a purely technical level, to reduce lags in adjusting factor stocks to factor adjustment costs of the sorts flagged under lock-in and lock-out.[4] It seems preferable, however, to retain lags as a distinct conceptual category. Because time is the key variable in dynamic theories, and because commitment is a dynamic theory, it is hard to think that much clarity would be gained by recasting lags in less temporal terms.

Inertia

The spotlight has fallen, so far, on the economics of factor adjustment as the cause of commitment. There is, however, a widespread presumption that organizations are prone, for psychological and sociological reasons, to preserve the strategic status quo to a greater extent than they would if they were simply maximizing payoffs subject to the constraints of lock-in, lock-out and lags. In other words, organizations are widely presumed to have a built-in bias toward inertia. This presumption is reflected in the fact that more tends to be written about the challenge of getting organizations to change than about the challenge of ossification.

Organizational inertia has been alleged, for instance, of Detroit's three big carmakers, General Motors (GM), Ford and Chrysler, all of whom took somewhere between one and three decades to respond to the U.S. market's shift from large cars to small ones. Some of their implicit commitment to large car strategies can be rationalized in the purely economic terms discussed above. They were stuck with factors whose value was specialized to the large car business. They lacked the know-how to adjust quickly to the shift toward smaller cars. And once they had lost the lead to foreign competitors, that locked them out of opportunities to invest profitably in the small car business. But it also seems that their loss of leadership was more than just a matter of optimally managed capitulation. It would be hard, for example, to explain GM's repeated failures, with the Vega subcompact in the early 1970s, the J-cars in the early 1980s and subsequently the Saturn project, to deliver cars as light and inexpensive as originally intended, without invoking *some* measure of organizational inertia. As the head of GM's largest division (who later became the company's president) confessed, "Chevrolet is such a big monster that you twist its tail and nothing happens at the other end for months and months."[5]

Discussions of organizational inertia mostly start and stop with sightings of the phenomenon. It is possible, however, to be more specific about its sources. To begin at the micro level, consider the four possible bases of choice depicted in Exhibit 2.5. It should be obvious how inactivity and routines tend to induce persistence. Principles, defined here as binding constraints that supersede cost-benefit calculations, will have the same effect to the extent that they are fixed. Finally, psychological experiments suggest that even when choice *is* calculated, it will be biased in ways that are likely to compound the economic sources of commitment discussed previously. Three commitment-escalating biases are particularly noteworthy. First, the sunk cost fallacy will tend to reinforce the lock-in implied by sticky factors (Kahneman and Tversky 1979). Second, if the path not taken is hard to recall for lack of vividness, that will exacerbate lock-out (Tversky and Kahneman 1981). Third, excessive discounting of future consequences will favor persistence over switching if switches are subject to significant time lags (Ainslie 1975).

Organizational theory suggests many reasons why these micro-sources of behavioral commitment might be expected to coalesce into macro ones. They include phenomena such as free-riding, defensiveness, logrolling and groupthink. A more coherent way, however, of seeing why extra persistence is likely to result from embedding individuals in organizations is to note that organizations

Exhibit 2.5 The Behavioral Bases of Choice

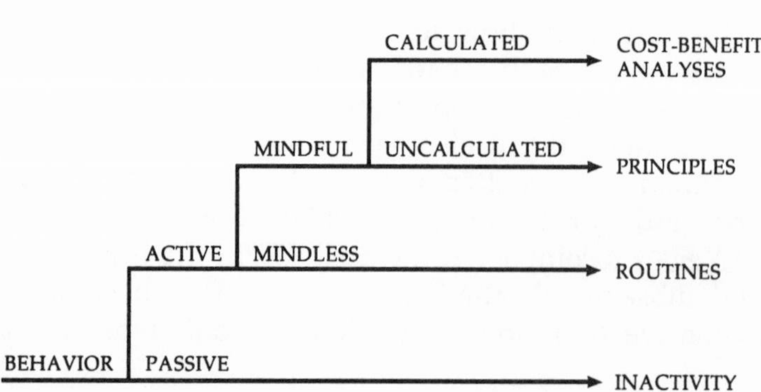

implicitly or explicitly substitute long-term contractual arrangements for market-mediated spot transactions among individuals. Since the latter arrangement maximizes the scope for adjustment to changing economic pressures, organizations must inhibit adjustment relative to market-mediated transactions if they are to serve any distinctive purpose.[6] In other words, a degree of inertial commitment is intrinsic to organizational coalitions.

Organizational inertia is often modeled in terms of a particular sort of durable, specialized, untraded factor that the organization is supposed to be stuck with, its *culture,* broadly construed (e.g., Deal and Kennedy 1982). There is less agreement about whether culture should be treated as a constraint or as a candidate for modification in line with the commitments the organization is contemplating. My personal sense is that while cultural differences can have a big influence on organizational performance (compare Wal-Mart and Sears, Roebuck), our understanding about how to transform "bad" cultures into "good" ones (about how to make Sears, Roebuck competitive with Wal-Mart) is too limited for us to treat culture as purely a choice variable. The accuracy of this assessment is immaterial to the framework for analyzing commitments to sticky factors that is developed in this book, but I *will* revisit it in the last section of the last chapter because of its broader importance.

To conclude this section, the tendency toward inertia, while common, is neither absolute nor uniform. Consider both qualifications in turn. First, the empirical evidence cited in the previous section suggests that while strategic stability is the rule, there are exceptions to it. There *are* periods when organizations unfreeze and adjust to changes in their environments. Second, thresholds of change seem to be highly idiosyncratic. Detroit's three big carmakers, for instance, probably had relatively high thresholds of change because they had traditionally emphasized making cars bigger and more expensive, because that strategy had worked in the past and because optimal adjustment required downsizing their organizations as well as their cars. They would probably have adjusted more quickly to the shift to small cars had they been less culture-bound, successful and conflicted.

Commitment is the only general explanation for sustained differences in the performance of organizations.

The previous chapter criticized the success factor approach for lacking generality in a particular sense: for failing to explain why losers don't simply close the gap with winners by stocking up on the same success factor(s). Commitment seems, unlike the swarm of success factors, to be both sufficient *and* necessary to explain sustained differences in the performance of organizations.

The argument for sufficiency has been made both theoretically and empirically. Systematic mathematical exploration of whether commitment can (under sophisticated as opposed to sleepy competition) lead to sustained performance differences started in the late 1970s. The stock of such mathematical models now runs into the thousands.[7] These models do not quite supplant the earlier literature on strategy because their stylized treatments of phenomena such as races, wars of attrition and bluffing are, of necessity, quite specialized. But collectively, they do suggest that commitment *can* drive a wedge between the performance of competing organizations, even if they are all smart about what they are up to. The reason is that when history matters, competitors that start out with different stocks of sticky factors may pursue different trajectories that partially insulate them from each other *even* if all of them remain perfectly alert to all market opportunities at all times.[8]

This theoretical conclusion about sufficiency is backstopped by the results of recent empirical research. These results favor the interpretation of sustained intraindustry performance differences in terms of the heterogeneity of the bundles of factors (relative strengths and weaknesses) that market rivals bring to bear in competing with each other. The bases of such heterogeneity are elaborated later in this book. What needs to be emphasized here is that a degree of commitment in regard to choices about such factors ensures that they can lead to sustained performance differences rather than merely transient ones.

Furthermore, commitment seems to be necessary as well as sufficient for sustained performance differences.[9] To see this, it is necessary to imagine a situation in which there is no lock-in, lock-out, lags or inertia. Since that may be hard to do, it is fortunate that economists have, under the rubric of perfect contestability, already performed that thought experiment for us.[10] They have concluded that without commitment, differences in the performance of organizations would be ironed out in the twinkling of an eye.

This theoretical argument can be illustrated with the example of the U.S. airline industry. The airline industry was deregulated at the insistence of contestability-minded econocrats who prophesied that if the regulations imposed on the industry in the 1930s were dismantled, zero (economic) profits would be earned all around. They reasoned that even if a particular city-pair route ended up being monopolized, that monopolist would be policed perfectly by the threat of "hit-and-run" entry implicit in zero commitment. The nature of that supposed threat can be made explicit. In the absence of inertia, many potential entrants would wait in the wings for profitable opportunities to undercut the incumbent monopolist. In the absence of lags, any such opportunities would be exploited instantaneously. In the absence of any degree of lock-out, entrants would be competitive with the incumbent, letting them profitably undercut any price that exceeded cost. And the absence of lock-in—of commitments of any sort to specific city-pairs—would mean that even if the monopolist tried to retaliate with predatory prices, entrants could simply fly out of harm's way. In the words of Alfred Kahn, chairman of the Civil Aeronautics Board in the late 1970s, and a key campaigner for its dissolution, airplanes were simply "marginal costs with wings."

Since deregulation, performance differentials within the airline industry have actually exceeded those in most other industries. Contestability has been impeded by the commitments the airlines have made to a range of sticky factors, particularly hubs and computer reservation systems (CRSs).[11] Hubs matter because hub-and-spoke operations are harder to attack than point-to-point operations. Attacks from the same hub are limited by the availability of gates and slots, which, in many cases, have been contracted out into the next century. Attacks from adjacent hubs are constrained by the fact that the prime sites, measured in terms of local enplanements and geographic centrality, all seem to have been spoken for. The proprietors of CRSs are protected, in addition, by the network economies that permit only a few such systems to be viable. In addition to generating substantial cash flow and increasing general marketing effectiveness, a successful CRS enhances the ability to monitor attacks and retaliate against them. To illustrate the difference that these commitments make, USAir earned operating margins roughly five times the industry average in the first decade after deregulation because of its fortress hub at Pittsburgh, and American did two-and-a-half times as well as the industry because of its ownership of SABRE, the most successful CRS, as well as the hubs that it developed at Dallas, Chicago and other locations. Pan American, in contrast, illustrates the dark side of commitment: it was stuck with an above-average proportion of wide-bodied aircraft unsuited to hub-and-spoke operations and was too late and too strapped for cash to mount a serious effort to develop a CRS. It has, as a result, lost money more years than not since deregulation.

The sticky factors that underpin sustained performance differences vary in their importance from industry to industry. It is useful, nonetheless, to group them into the three broad classes of capacity, customer base and knowledge. Theory suggests that competition over these three classes of factors should take somewhat different forms. It also supports the plausible inference that industries in which customer bases and (especially) knowledge are important will offer more scope for "strategizing" than commodity industries in which capacity tends to be the dominant factor and "economizing" the dominant logic.[12] While some industries (e.g., the airline industry) cannot be classified thus, the empirical evidence indicates that at least in the manufacturing sector, most industries can be sorted relatively cleanly into these categories, with capital-intensity, advertising-intensity and R&D-intensity serving as proxies for the importance of the three classes of sticky factors. For example, analysis by Collis (1990) that is reproduced in Exhibit 2.6 indicates that out of 20 broad manufacturing sectors, six account for 75% of the manu-

Exhibit 2.6 The Distribution of Commitment-Intensive and Extensive Industries

A. CAPITAL-INTENSIVE SECTORS		B. ADVERTISING-INTENSIVE SECTORS	
Food processing	15%	Food products	26%
Textile fabrics	15%	Consumer chemical products	12%
Basic metals	13%	Misc. consumer products*	9%
Stone and clay products	13%	Household durables	7%
Basic chemicals	12%	Carpets, etc.**	6%
Pulp and paper	8%	Glass and ceramic products	5%
Subtotal	75%		65%

C. R&D-INTENSIVE SECTORS		D. COMMITMENT-EXTENSIVE SECTORS	
Machinery	26%	Clothing	24%
Electrical equipment	21%	Metalworking	14%
Chemicals	15%	Printing	10%
Transportation equipment	11%	Furniture	9%
Scientific equipment	9%	Woodworking	6%
Food products	5%	Stationery	5%
Subtotal	88%		68%

*SIC Code 39
**SIC Code 22

NOTE: Numbers may not add up exactly due to rounding errors.
SOURCE: Collis (1990).

facturing industries that rank in the top one-third in terms of capital-intensity, six for 65% of the top third in terms of advertising-intensity and six for 88% of the top third in terms of R&D-intensity.[13] Some strategists have arrived at similar industry classifications inductively (e.g., Williams 1988).

Exhibit 2.6 also indicates that industries not on any of these three lists tend to cluster as well: 68% of them are concentrated in six of the 20 sectors. These industries seem, at the time the data were generated, to have offered relatively limited commitment opportunities. My sense, however, is that it would be a serious error to ignore commitment even in environments that appear to be commitment-extensive instead of intensive. For one thing, theory suggests that apparently small deviations from the assumptions of perfect contestability can lead to commitment opportunities with significant performance implications. For another, the experience of the airline industry since deregulation serves as a reminder that smart competitors can, at least on occasion, turn commitment-extensive industries into commitment-intensive ones. Finally, choice would be trivial in the absence of commitment. This last point is elaborated in the next section.

The irreversibility implicit in commitment necessitates a deep look into the future.

The final criticism leveled in the first chapter against the success factor approach to strategy concerned its lack of *raison d'être*. It implicitly assumed but failed to explain why organizations need to think things through in considerable depth (as is usually urged in the literature on strategy). Commitment, in contrast, explicitly suggests a need for looking before leaping: for trying to peer into the future before it becomes the present.

That need can be flushed out, once again, with a thought experiment concerning the consequences of zero commitment. Imagine an organization pondering a capital investment. Assume, provisionally, that capital that is acquired today can subsequently be traded on a well-functioning market, that no future opportunities will be foregone as a result of the current choice, that the acquisition and deployment of capital involves negligible time lags, and that the organization is alert to its own objectives in making its choices. Kenneth Arrow (1964) has shown that such an organization will (optimally) invest in capital to the point where its *instantaneous* marginal productivity equals its costs.

Appearances notwithstanding, this is more than just another marginal rule of marginal interest. It has the striking implication that absent commitment, "The [optimal] decision as to the stock of capital to be held at any instant of time is myopic, being independent of future developments in technology, demand, or anything else; forecasts for only the most immediate future are needed, and then only as to capital goods prices" (Arrow 1968, p. 3). At a theoretical level, the myopic rule supersedes the usual logic of stacking up the present value of all future returns from an investment against its costs. At a practical level, it implies that organizations wouldn't need to take a long-term view. They wouldn't hatch multiyear plans that are the norm at most large companies. They wouldn't, in fact, even have to deliberate: they would simply try out the course of action that happened to look the most attractive at decision time. Thus, Reynolds would have shut the Hurricane Creek refinery as soon as it ran into red ink. And Boeing, Coors and General Motors wouldn't have had to think through their costly investment programs in any depth.

The advisability of totally discounting the future strains common sense. In subsequent work, Arrow (1968) examined this credibility gap and concluded that the optimality of myopia depends on the assumption that investment is reversible, because that lets the organization buy capital, derive its marginal product for an arbitrarily short time span and then resell it (possibly at a different price). Irreversibility, he noted, invalidates this myopic line of reasoning; in particular, he emphasized that if disinvestment is disallowed, an alert organization may refrain from investment that is attractive in myopic terms if it anticipates that it would want to disinvest in the future. Disallowing disinvestment is, of course, a way to model lock-in. The three other sources of commitment discussed above also create a need to look beyond the present into the future. If future opportunities will be foregone as a consequence of doing one thing as opposed to another, the implied opportunity costs must be accounted for. If significant time lags are anticipated in doing something, it is clearly future rather than present market conditions that are relevant to the choice about whether to do it all. Finally, organizational inertia implies a need to look into the future because it suggests that the current choice may influence the quality of future ones.

Two points should stand out from this discussion. First, commitment, unlike the success factor approach, *does* suggest a need for looking before leaping, for thinking things through ahead of time. Second, that need stems from the irreversibility that is implicit in the concept of commitment; as Ortega pointed out, commitment makes it costly to change one's mind. The connection with irreversibility is cardinal because it seems to underpin commitment's ability to beat all known success factors on all four criteria introduced in the first chapter and reviewed in this one: identification, concreteness, generality and necessity. Strategic theories that trade on success factors are essentially static. Commitment is a superior way of thinking about strategy not just because it is a dynamic theory, but because it is *the* dynamic theory implied by irreversibility. Irreversibility is simply a recognition of the fact that the arrow of time points away from the past and toward the future.[14] The unidirectionality of time seems fundamental enough to serve as the foundation of strategy, one that may finally allow the field to progress like a normal (i.e., cumulative) science.

Summary

This chapter defined commitment as the tendency of organizations to persist with their respective strategies. Commitment has four possible causes: lock-in, lock-out, lags and inertia. Without commitment, there would be neither persistent differences in organizations' performance levels nor any need to anticipate the future. The next chapter discusses how managers can use the concept of commitment to improve the quality of choices that they make.

3

→⟫ ⟪←

Choice: Making Commitments

> A decision to build the Edsel or Mustang (or locate your new factory in Orlando or Yakima) shouldn't be made hastily; nor without plenty of inputs. . . . [But there is] no point in taking three weeks to make a decision that can be made in three seconds—and corrected inexpensively later if wrong. The whole organization may be out of business while you oscillate between baby-blue or buffalo-brown coffee cups.
>
> —Robert Townsend, *Up the Organization*

Chapter 2 highlighted the strategic salience of commitment. It concluded with the observation that commitment creates a need to look deep into the future. How should managers spread their limited capacity for in-depth attention across the choices they have to make? To answer that question, it is useful to distinguish among choices in terms of the commitment they embody: between, as Robert Townsend put it, choices about new products or factories and choices about the color of the coffee cups in the company cafeteria. Choices of the former sort can reasonably be anticipated to have a greater impact on the future. They are therefore the ones that should be analyzed in depth, i.e., in light of the strategic factor of commitment.

This chapter elaborates on these points. It uses, as a running example, Honda's drive to dominance in the U.S. market for motor-

Exhibit 3.1 U.S. Motorcycle Sales

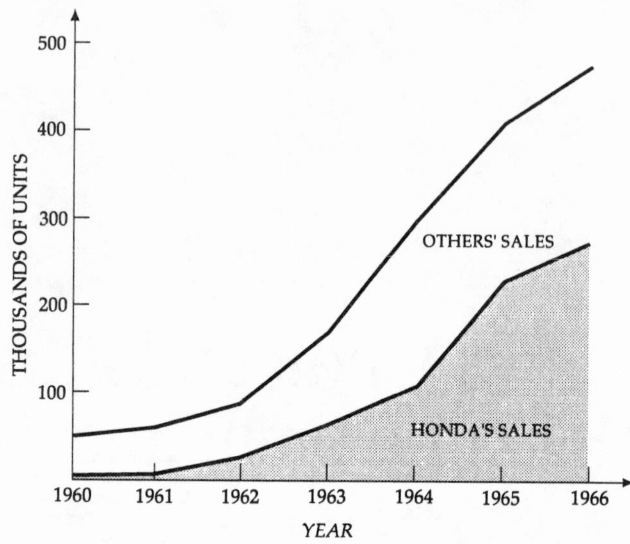

cycles. Honda established a marketing subsidiary in the United States in 1959; by 1966, its lightweight bikes accounted for nearly two-thirds of all the motorcycles sold there (see Exhibit 3.1). There has been considerable controversy about what happened at Honda, and what it means for strategy. Commitment theory's ability to cut through this controversy is a useful empirical supplement to the conceptual arguments developed below.

Commitment complicates choice.

In what sense can commitment be said to complicate choice? The most obvious answer is that accounting for it requires guessing the future, which is hard. There must be more to it, however, than that. Commitment is not alone in requiring predictions about the consequences of current actions: predictions are also required to put other theories of strategy into practice.

To see how commitment *distinctively* complicates choice, reconsider the thought experiment discussed in the last section of the previous chapter, concerning an organization contemplating a capital investment. Arrow (1964) noted that with zero commitment, the organization could buy capital, derive its marginal product for an arbitrarily short time and then resell it. Under such conditions, the choice about whether or not to invest would require a prediction about just one thing: the price(s), in the most immediate future, of the factor(s) being invested in. On analyzing the case of perfectly irreversible rather than reversible investment, Arrow (1968) found that the optimal investment policy would require predictions about many more things (the evolution of demand, technology and the supply of other factors), and farther out into the future too. This can safely be described as a complication relative to the zero-commitment case.

The results of the thought experiment can be restated more generally. Commitment complicates choice because it explicitly recognizes that some of the factors in the organizational coalition are not traded on well-functioning markets. Because of such factor market imperfections, expectations about what the future holds in store cannot be collapsed into a simple prediction of tomorrow's factor prices. The explosion that results in the number and futurity of the predictions required for in-depth analysis has been tagged as the curse of dimensionality. The curse has three components. First, more extensive predictions clearly require the generation of more information. Second, uncertainty mounts as one tries to look farther out into the future, swelling the number of contingencies that must somehow be accounted for. Third, interactions among the variables whose values are to be predicted imply that future dynamics may have a *nonlinear* (i.e., *very complicated*) structure.[1]

All these complications are evident in the Honda case. The move into the United States involved commitment because many of the factors required to compete there could not be bought and sold on perfect markets. In-depth analysis of the move therefore had to attend to demand, cost and competitive dynamics in that market. The future values of the relevant parameters were, however, enshrouded in uncertainty: Honda knew very little about the U.S. market back in the 1950s. And these parameters would interact, possibly in nonlinear ways, to influence the aggregate value of a drive toward dominance. No wonder Honda had its work cut out for it.

Orthodox approaches to choice do not help managers cope with commitment.

Much has been written about the complexities that surround choice when the (factor) price system is suspect. Little has been provided, however, in the way of practical succor. The bulk of the previous literature fails to be helpful because it clusters, from the perspective of commitment, around one of two poles.[2] At one pole, each choice is supposed to be looked at in considerable depth; at the other, none is. Both poles are inhospitable to practitioners, but for different reasons: the first one optimistically assumes that they can aspire to comprehensive rationality; the second one pessimistically presumes that they cannot outperform automata. Consider them in more detail.

The Optimistic Pole

At the optimistic pole, each choice is supposed to be assessed in depth. The conceptual appeal of taking such a comprehensive approach to commitment should be obvious. If it were only practical! A dialogue from Galsworthy's (1932, p. 24) *The Flowering Wilderness* captures both the underpinnings of this approach and its unwieldiness. He: "I take each problem as it comes, I do the sum, I return the answer, and so I act." She: "That means doing so long a sum every time that I can't think how you ever get to acting." In other words, common sense suggests that a policy of analyzing each and every choice in depth fails to reckon with the complexities created by commitment and is therefore precluded by bounds on managers' abilities to acquire, absorb and act upon information about the future.

Such considerations notwithstanding, the Boston Consulting Group (1975) has offered an essentially optimistic interpretation of the happenings at Honda. According to BCG, Honda thought through all the choices it would face in the United States (about product mix, distribution, advertising and so on), devised a strategy of using its low-cost position in lightweight bikes (where costs mattered most) to create a huge pool of demand for lightweights in the United States, and stuck by that strategy in making the choices that it did. Actually, Honda did nothing of the sort. The initial choice of product mix, for instance, is recalled as follows by the first president of American Honda (Pascale 1984, pp. 54–55):

> Mr. Honda was especially confident of the 250cc and 305cc machines. The shape of the handlebar on these larger machines looked like the eyebrow of Buddha, which he felt was a strong selling point. Thus, after some discussion and with no compelling criteria for selection, we configured our start-up inventory with 25 percent of each of our four products—the 50cc Supercub and

Exhibit 3.2 Honda's Early Revisions in the United States

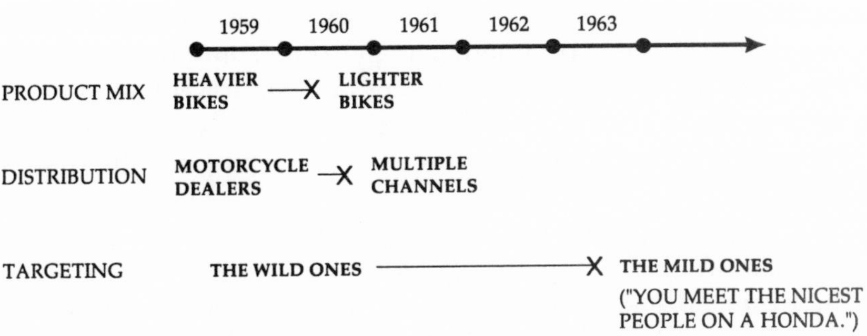

> the 125cc, 250cc and 305cc machines. In dollar value terms, of course, the inventory was heavily weighted toward the larger bikes.

Even more interestingly, if Honda *had* taken the sort of approach suggested by BCG, it would probably have done itself a disservice. Note that Honda quickly reversed most of its initial choices in the United States as it learned more about the market there (Exhibit 3.2). If it had set an overarching U.S. strategy and stuck to it, it probably wouldn't have uncovered the latent demand for lightweight bikes that it subsequently rode to fame and fortune. By implication, overoptimism about managers' capacities for in-depth analysis can easily backfire.

The Pessimistic Pole

At the pessimistic pole, no choices are supposed to be assessed in depth. This certainly simplifies matters. But it has the awkward consequence of throwing out the baby (the strategic factor of commitment) with the bathwater (the complexities that it creates). Chapters 1 and 2 should have established commitment as the right way to think about strategy. This chapter has suggested, so far, that commitment is what places a premium on (some) in-depth analysis in the first place. To turn one's back on in-depth analysis anyway is to imply that the only strategic factor identified as possibly useful, commitment, is actually useless because it complicates choice too much.

While the complexities wrought by commitment probably put the first-best solution, of all-inclusive in-depth analysis, out of reach, the pessimistic pole seems to settle for less than the second-best solution when it succumbs, in effect, to myopia. That is, at least, what numerical and experimental analyses of commitment suggest.[3] Myopic policies tend, under conditions of commitment, to underperform first-best ones by a wide margin. That leaves lots of room, presumably, to beat myopia without overreaching for the first-best solution.

Pascale (1984) has, nonetheless, offered an essentially pessimistic interpretation of the happenings at Honda. The revisions alluded to in Exhibit 3.2 suggest to Pascale that Honda's success in the United States was mostly attributable to "miscalculation, mistakes, and serendipitous events *outside its field of vision*" (p. 57), and that the company deserves credit only for abiding by the allegedly Japanese "belief that corporate direction evolves from an incremental adjustment to unfolding events" (p. 64). All of this is meant to take a poke at BCG's interpretation: Pascale claims that Honda did well by *not* thinking through any particular choice in great depth.

This vision of a Japanese tortoise beating Western hares does not, however, quite cross the finish line. If Honda had just been incrementing along, it probably wouldn't have moved so early into the U.S. market in the first place. There was nothing easy or obvious about Honda's move to diversify geographically when it did: unlike other Japanese companies that were quick to move overseas, it held a dominant domestic position in its only major product, motorcycles; it also had its hands full trying to get into car manufacture before Japan's Ministry of International Trade and Industry (MITI) lowered the boom on further entry into that field. In addition, the overseas debut in the United States contradicted conventional wisdom and the wishes of MITI and the Japanese trading companies that had previously handled Honda's limited exports to Southeast Asia. Honda nevertheless chose to emphasize direct sales to the United States instead of sales to Southeast Asia through the trading companies because of its founders' strong sense that the size and level of development of the United States made it the *leading market:* that products had to succeed there if they were to win really wide international acceptance (Sakiya 1982). This doesn't sound the least bit like myopia.

To sum up, neither of the two polar perspectives on choice described in this section is of much help to managers who must cope with the complexities commitment introduces into choice. What is needed pragmatically, as opposed to optimistically or pessimistically, is something quite different. The quest for it is aided by a clue: both of the polar perspectives tend to treat in-depth analysis very evenhandedly, as equally desirable or undesirable in all instances. From the perspective of commitment theory, such analytical evenhandedness makes sense only if individual choices wield similar degrees of influence on the organization's future direction, i.e., are apt to be equally commitment-intensive. The next section shows that this is not so; the sections that follow discuss the implications.

Commitment is mostly concentrated in a few choices.

Is commitment spread fairly evenly among the choices in the typical organizational sequence, or do a few choices embody much more commitment than all the rest? The Honda case inclines one toward the latter position, since the move into the United States was less easily reversible than many of the moves Honda made once it got there. So, too, does the broader panorama of Honda's history. Consider just the company's first two decades. Between 1952 and 1954, Honda made a substantial investment—equal to thirty times its paid-up capital—in importing machine tools which it modified to run at unprecedented speeds and tolerances. In the late 1950s, it built the largest motorcycle plant in the world, moved into the United States, and entered the much bigger game of car manufacture. And in the late 1960s, it bet its embattled car business on the development of a cleaner engine technology by putting other development efforts on hold for several years. Each of these choices evidently embodied much more than a modal level of commitment.

More generally, the idea that commitment is typically concentrated in a few key choices is consistent with the evidence on the piecewise continuity of strategies (patterns of behavior) presented in chapter 2. If many of the choices in the typical sequence embodied significant individual commitment (in terms of their potential for changing the organization's direction), strategies would bounce around more. And if none of the choices in the typical sequence embodied significant individual commitment, strategies would shift smoothly over time. So the available evidence on the dynamics of strategies strongly suggests that the typical commitment sequence consists of many small steps punctuated by a few large ones. There are several reasons why small isn't *always* beautiful—why it is occasionally necessary to move in large steps or not at all.

Indivisibilities

By indivisibilities, I mean that it may be more efficient, in a purely technical sense, to move in one step rather than in several smaller ones. Indivisibilities can operate at either the level of individual factors or across factors. At the former level, it is possible that factors can efficiently be added or removed only in lumps of *minimum* fixed size, implying the suboptimality of trying to work with smaller increments. Reconsider the large steps that Honda took. An irreducible degree of lumpiness is evident in efficient motorcycle manufacturing facilities, a viable presence overseas and in car manufacture, and the development of a radically new engine technology.

Indivisibilities across factors, previously referred to as factor complementarities, make a few choices stand out in a rather different way. Arrow (1974) suggested that fixed costs are incurred in reorganizing, i.e., in destroying or resurrecting factor complementarities. To the extent that such fixed costs are substantial, they imply the efficiency of contemplating broad changes of direction rarely rather than all the time. Evidence assembled by Miller and Friesen (1984) attests to the role of this effect in accounting for the general infrequency of strategic change.[4]

Speed

It is often quicker to move in one large step rather than several smaller ones. In extreme cases, large steps can even be *infinitely* quicker: if Honda hadn't rushed into car manufacture, it probably wouldn't have been able to get in at all. Considerations of speed are related to indivisibilities in the same way that the lead times in adjusting factor stocks are related to factor adjustment costs: while the first quantity can be reduced, in a technical sense, to the second one, it is hard to imagine that recasting temporal effects in less temporal terms will add to the clarity of the dynamic theory being developed in this book. Speed will therefore be retained as a separate explanation of the possible benefits of moving in large steps rather than small ones.

At an internal level, speed derives its value from the organizational tendency toward inertia. Organizational inertia in the face of environmental changes typically creates a pent-up need for strategic change by the time that possibility surfaces on the organizational agenda. A pent-up need for change places, by definition, some premium on speed once change becomes possible. Miller and Friesen's (1984) evidence is, once again, suggestive of the importance of this effect.[5]

At an external level, speed can be valuable because of the character of interactions with other players. Suppose that there are opportunities, perhaps because of environmental shocks such as shifts in technology, demand, input availability, regulation or the structures of adjacent industries, to acquire or develop factors at costs less than their "fair" values. Competition to lock into undervalued factors typically means that the bargain will be short-lived. Moving quickly to exploit particular bargains may then be the only way the organization can hope to create value. Remember the lesson of contestability theory: those who commit not cannot hope to make money; by staying out of the competitive fray, they simply avoid losing it. Honda certainly seems to have realized this in taking the large steps that it did.

Self-stabilization

Last but not least, the two levels of action implicit in the distinction between large and small steps are essential if the organization is to adapt to *unforeseen* changes in its environment. Note the ease, in principle, of designing a system that can adapt to foreseeable environmental changes. A simple feedback loop that relates results to actions in a preprogrammed way will suffice. The real challenge is to design a system that can stabilize itself after being disturbed in a way unforeseen by and uncongenial to its initial programming. In the face of such disturbances, action at a higher level to reprogram the system is required. In other words, a self-stabilizing organization must contain (at least) two distinct decision-making loops that are linked hierarchically to one another. Note that this implies a *qualitative* distinction, between higher-level choices concerning the fundamental variables that govern the organization and lower-level choices that take those variables to be fixed.[6] The way they interact over time is that higher-level choices impose constraints on lower-level actions, and lower-level choices provide the necessary feedback to reevaluate higher-level actions.

Systems theorists have shown, in addition, that self-stabilization also requires the higher-level loop to induce changes less frequently than the lower-level loop. As Ashby (1956, p. 219) originally put it, "If it takes ten years to observe adequately the effect of a profound re-organization of a Civil Service, then such re-organizations ought not to occur more frequently than at eleven-year intervals." The picture that emerges is of a lower-level feedback loop that is active most of the time and relates results to actions in a preprogrammed way, and a higher-level loop that is dormant most of the time but occasionally rewires the first feedback loop, i.e., changes the organization's strategy. The next section argues that large commitments should be thought of, in this context, as switches that trigger higher-level consideration as a possible prelude to changes in strategy.

Attention should be focused on commitment-intensive (strategic) choices

The large-scale structure of commitment sequences is generally thought, for all the reasons recited in the last section, to consist of a few key choices that each involve significant commitment and very many more that do not. That suggests a third way of allocating limited managerial capacity for in-depth analysis among choices, one that cannot really be lined up between the two conventional poles: focus on the few choices that involve significant individual commitment, as Honda's co-founders did. They paid much more attention to the choice of where, if at all, to push overseas than to all the specific choices that would flow therefrom. They appointed a task force to help them make that higher-level choice. After visiting all significant non-communist markets, it recommended that Honda bypass the United States. The co-founders, particularly Takeo Fujisawa, reflected at length on the task force's recommendations and finally rejected them because of a strong sense that they did not fully capture the much greater upside potential in the U.S. market. Subsequent choices about how to compete in the U.S. market were, in contrast, delegated: the Honda executive most knowledgeable about the U.S. market was summoned, reminded of the stakes for the company and the constraints on its exposure there, and asked to do what he could.

This way of allocating limited managerial attention among choices is, I should stress, more than just a rediscovery of the familiar distinction between strategic and tactical choices. The conventional wisdom that some choices are much more important than all the rest does not quite settle where a specific choice fits into the schema.

This is the question von Clausewitz (1833, p. 128) bailed out on in his classic definition of strategy:

> The distinction between tactics and strategy is now almost universal, and everyone knows fairly well where each particular factor belongs without clearly understanding why. Whenever such categories are blindly used, there must be a deep-seated reason for it. We have tried to discover the distinction, and have to say that it was just this common usage that led to it.

Contemporary strategists have tried to be more specific about the sorts of choices that should be treated as strategic, but have clung to disciplinary lines in doing so. Industrial economists have, for obvious reasons, focused on the industries in which the organization competes, i.e., on choices such as diversification and vertical integration. Business strategists have been more prone to take the organization's presence in a particular industry—the existence of a business—as given, and to emphasize that choices about *how* to compete (''generic strategies'') can be as strategic as choices about *where* to compete. Organizational theorists end up flagging many of the same choices as strategic, but define them in terms of major changes in the relation of the organization to its environment. And so on.

Commitment theory suggests a way of distinguishing strategic and tactical choices that is less dependent on disciplinary prejudices. According to the theory, commitment-intensive choices are the ones that should be treated as strategic, i.e., looked at in extra depth. There are three reasons why it makes sense to think about strategic importance in terms of commitment-intensity.

Impact

Choices that individually embody significant commitment are crucial in the sense that they have the most potential to influence the organization's future opportunities. It is particularly important to take the right path at such forks. In other words, commitment-intensive choices can be counted on to have a disproportionately large impact on future performance. This extra impact demands extra attention, in the form of in-depth analysis.

The point of the analysis, it should be emphasized, is *not* to consider a single choice in isolation. Instead, it is to reassess the organization's strategic options—the overall courses of action available to it—at a time when that is particularly likely to prove productive. Commitment-intensive choices are timely in this regard because they represent potential turning points. In addition, the extent to which they predetermine the choices that follow alleviates the complexities of predicting the future (see the first section of this chapter).

From this perspective, Honda's co-founders deserve credit principally for realizing, before research on international business (e.g., Aharoni 1966) told us so, that the location and the timing of the company's first thrust overseas are likely to have a significant impact on its subsequent international development. Not everyone possesses such marvelous intuition. But everyone, we will see, can use commitment theory to identify the choices that are worth thinking through in depth.

Identifiability

To understand why commitment-intensity is a practical as well as theoretically sound way of defining strategic importance, replay the Honda tape. Even a nonvirtuoso could have used commitment theory to figure out, ahead of time, that Honda's move overseas was important enough to be looked at in depth. The move into the United States involved significant sunk costs for a company that had only $50 million in annual sales at the time. By offending MITI, it increased the chances that Honda would be denied the opportunity to manufacture cars. Significant lead times could be expected because it takes years to consummate foreign entries. And the move symbolized to everyone within the organization Honda's intention of becoming a world-class competitor. Because of its commitment-intensity in all these respects, the move overseas could have been spotted as strategic back when it was being contemplated and analyzed in depth. Compare this with BCG's and Pascale's perspectives on the happenings at Honda, neither of which places any *particular* emphasis on the choice about moving into the United States, starting in Southeast Asia or staying at home.

The commitment-based procedure used to identify the strategic choice in the Honda case can be generalized. Chapter 2's concreteness about the causes of commitment helps in this regard. It suggests that a choice is strategic if it involves significant sunk costs, opportunity costs, lead times or symbolism. There is an obvious correspondence between the first three of these measures and the three economic causes of commitment that were discussed in chapter 2: lock-in, lock-out and lags. The symbolism of a choice measures its effect on the organization's culture, defined broadly to encompass the organization's values, heroes, myths and rituals (Deal and Kennedy 1982, p. 4). Highly symbolic choices are likely to have a significant impact on the inertial component of the organization's strategy, which was the fourth cause of commitment discussed in chapter 2.

Unless one of the options on the table scores high on at least one of these four measures, a choice cannot have much of an impact on the future. In practice, strategic choices usually show up as such on more than one of the four measures, for the same reason that the four causes of commitment tend to intertwine.

The interrelation of the four measures of commitment-intensity facilitates advance recognition of the choices that should be looked at in depth. So does the fact that these measures, unlike previous ones, are explicitly based on *the* strategic factor, commitment. Of course, not even these four commitment-based measures will pick up, *ex ante,* all the choices that turn out to be consequential *ex post.* It is always possible to imagine unlikely sequences of events transforming apparently insignificant choices into significant ones: the loss of a battle for want of a horseshoe nail is perhaps the classic example. Having noted this possibility, I do not see that there is anything to be gained by harping on it. Commitment-based measures of strategic importance may not work perfectly, but they do seem to be the best ones around. The trick is to strike the appropriate trade-off between two kinds of error: treating strategic choices as nonstrategic and nonstrategic choices as strategic. This sort of trade-off is discussed at length in chapter 7.

Integration

In spite of the above-average impact of commitment-intensive choices and their usual identifiability, it would be inadvisable to focus on them if it were impossible to reconcile in-depth attention to a few choices with shallow attention to the remainder. Fortunately, the literature on systems control, which was discussed above, implies the feasibility of such integration. Recall the chief lesson of that literature: that the capability of adjusting to unforeseen environmental changes requires two feedback loops, one of which can reprogram or reset the context for the other, and will do so on occasion. The distinction between commitment-intensive choices and garden-variety choices maps neatly into this hierarchical structure. Commitment-intensive choices set, by virtue of their greater irreversibility, the context for the far more numerous and less commitment-intensive choices that follow them, at least until the next big one comes along. Since commitment-intensive choices are infrequent, the contextuating effect tends to be as significant in general as it proved in the case of Honda's move into the United States. It is therefore safe to associate commitment-intensive choices with the higher-level feedback loop of the two identified by systems theory. There is, as a result, no inconsistency in simultaneously using commitment-intensive choices to reconsider the programming of the system and making the myriad choices that do not fit into that category in preprogrammed, or relatively mindless, ways.

In terms of Exhibit 2.5's classification of the behavioral bases of choice, choices that aren't commitment-intensive should be made largely by default or routine. Commitment-intensive (or strategic) choices qualify, in contrast, for treatment mindful of their deep implications. From Exhibit 2.5, mindful treatments can attempt either to discover and apply the principle relevant to the (strategic) choice at hand or to calculate, via cost-benefit analysis, the values afforded by the various (strategic) options. The balance to be struck between the two in making commitment-intensive choices, which will be described without further fanfare as strategic, is the topic of the next section.

Strategic choices demand cost-benefit analysis.

In order to understand the balance to be struck between principles and cost-benefit analysis in strategic choices, it is useful to begin by sharpening the distinction between the two. Prelec (1991) has done so with admirable clarity:

> Essential to the application of a principle is the belief that a principle does not *supplement* ordinary cost-benefit analysis, but rather *replaces* it (Etzioni, 1988). In other words, by invoking a principle one does not add another consideration onto what Janis and Mann (1977) call the "decisional balance-sheet," but instead discards the balance-sheet altogether. By a rule or principle, then, I refer to any behavioral policy that overrides a cost-benefit calculation.

Exhibit 3.3 Qualitative Cost-Benefit Analysis

In the Affair of so much Importance to you, wherein you ask my Advice, I cannot for want of sufficient Premises, advise you what to determine, but if you please, I will tell you *how*. When these difficult Cases occur, they are difficult chiefly because while we have them under Consideration all the Reasons *pro* and *con* are not present to the Mind at the same time, but sometimes one Set present themselves, and at other times another, the first being out of Sight. Hence the various Purposes or Inclinations that alternatively prevail, and the Uncertainty that perplexes us. To get over this, my Way is, to divide half a Sheet of Paper by a Line into two Columns, writing over the one *Pro*, and over the other *Con*. Then during three or four Days Consideration, I put down under the different Heads short Hints of the different Motives that at different Times occur to me for or against the Measure. When I have thus got them all together in one View, I endeavor to estimate their respective Weights; and where I find two, one on each side, that seem equal, I strike them both out; If I find a Reason *pro* equal to some two Reasons *con*, I strike out the three. If I judge some two Reasons *con* equal to some three Reasons *pro*, I strike out five, and thus proceeding I find at length where the Balance lies; and if after a Day or two of farther Consideration nothing new that is of Importance occurs on either side, I come to a Determination accordingly. And tho' the Weight of Reasons cannot be taken with the Precision of Algebraic Quantities, yet when each is thus considered separately and comparatively, and the whole lies before me, I think I can judge better, and am less likely to make a rash Step; and in fact I have found great Advantage from this kind of Equation, in what may be called *Moral* or *Prudential Algebra*.

--Benjamin Franklin, *Letter to Joseph Priestley*

At least two aspects of this description deserve to be elaborated. First of all, cost-benefit analysis should not be confused with the much narrower notion of quantitative analysis. Cost-benefit analysis is "calculated" in the sense that it involves trade-offs across different dimensions of value, pro and con. These trade-offs may be quantitative. But they may also be qualitative, as suggested in Benjamin Franklin's letter to Joseph Priestley (see Exhibit 3.3). Second, while cost-benefit analysis can always accommodate another line item on the balance sheet of pros and cons, principles tend to be absolute in the sense that they are supposed to preempt other considerations whenever they kick in. The principle of outpacing one's competitor(s) (see Gilbert and Strebel 1988, p. 74) is a popular example. Note that it leaves little or no room for the cost-benefit analysis of the individual choices it is supposed to overshadow.

This book places its bets on cost-benefit analysis. One reason is that it seems to be difficult, if not impossible, to come up with principles that are reasonably specific *and* make sense all the time. Etzioni (1988, ch. 10) elaborates on this problem; all I will do is illustrate it in the context of the principle I just mentioned. Economic analysis shows that the principle of staying ahead of one's competitors *never* makes collective sense and can be individually rational all around only in the presence of *strategic complementarities* that make it optimal to respond to attacks (concessions) by competitors with attacks (concessions) of one's own. While many market games are governed by strategic complementarities, many (perhaps most) are not.[7] To make matters worse, we lack simple principles for distinguishing situations subject to strategic complementarities from those that are not: it all seems to depend on the specifics of the situation (Bulow, Geanakoplos and Klemperer 1985). This does not qualify as evidence of the efficacy of principles.

Second, irrespective of how cost-benefit analysis and principles compare in absolute terms, cost-benefit analysis does seem to have a comparative advantage at handling *strategic* (commitment-intensive) choices. To see this, begin by considering what we have learned from research on choice by a single person. The only systematic argument that principles might outperform cost-benefit analysis depends on the drop-in-the-bucket effects of choices that are individually small and frequent, such as smoking one more cigarette (Herrnstein and Prelec 1991). Principles seem to be disadvantaged, in contrast, in dealing with choices that are individually important and infrequent, i.e., strategic. Individual importance and infrequency result in idiosyncracy, which complicates the sort of reasoning by analogy that underlies analysis by principles. It is hard, for instance, to see how reasoning by analogy could have helped Honda make the right call in 1959: it had no experience then of the U.S. market, and the most obvious precedent, Toyota's attempt to export Toyopet cars there, had just been judged an abysmal failure.

Recognition of the multiperson context of most strategic choices within organizations further tips the appropriate balance of attention away from principles and toward cost-benefit analysis. For one thing, principles, unlike cost-benefit analyses, cannot be audited. Lack of auditability invites all sorts of distortions in multiperson settings. For another, different people will, even in the same situation, often favor different principles. Conflicts are particularly likely if a choice impinges on more than one organizational subunit, as many strategic choices tend to. Analysis by principles founders on such conflicts; cost-benefit analysis, in contrast, does not because it is willing to make trade-offs among everything, including conflicting principles.

To say that strategic choices demand cost-benefit analysis is not to deny the possible usefulness of principles. The articulation of principles may help prevent choice-by-choice analyses from nibbling away at the coherence of the organization's overall course of action. Such coherence will be particularly valuable when strategy implementation requires extensive coordination across functions or other organizational subunits (Porter 1985), or when the commitments involved are distributed smoothly over many choices instead of being concentrated in a few (Baldwin and Clark 1990). Even in such situations, however, the (higher-level) choice of an overarching strategic principle should surely be based on cost-benefit analysis, not on prejudice.

THE COST-BENEFIT ANALYSIS OF STRATEGIC CHOICES CAN PARTLY BE SYSTEMATIZED.

From the last section, the purpose of looking carefully at strategic choices—choices likely to have a material influence on the organization's future bundle of durable, specialized, untraded factors—is to net out the costs and the benefits of the possible courses of action so that they can be ranked. It often makes more sense to rank a few discrete options than the entire spectrum that may be possible. The process can be split into option generation and option evaluation, although the two often interact.

While it helps to focus on specific choices, the generation of the strategic options that are to be evaluated remains a creative task that cannot completely be systematized. That is not meant to disparage the importance of the task: the introduction of a new option can often resolve apparent choice dilemmas (e.g., Howard 1966). New options sometimes represent entirely new ideas. In many other instances, however, they recombine existing ones. One way to think through the combinatorial possibilities is to list respects in which options might differ, such as whether they represent change or continuity, whether they involve investment, disinvestment or both, the sorts of sticky factors involved, the scale and scope of the commitment(s) contemplated and the pace of commitment. Differences in such respects can be combined to generate different options. Usually, only a few of the combinations that are mathematically possible will fit together in a way that makes sense, reducing the number of options that need to be analyzed further.

The problem of evaluating the options that have been generated, while still complex, can be approached much more systematically. I discuss it in four steps that correspond to the remaining chapters of this book. The first step, which is the subject of chapter 4, involves comparing the strategic options available to the organization in terms of the *positioning* they imply, the difference between the costs that will be incurred by the organization and the benefits it will deliver to buyers under each strategic option. Comparisons with competitors often facilitate the comparison of strategic options in these terms. In addition to supplying a baseline for further analysis, positioning analysis flushes out the activities that will have to be performed if the targeted competitive position is to be achieved.

Positioning analysis, taken by itself, would favor options that promised superior positions. It is an incomplete basis for strategic choice because valuable product market positions are vulnerable (to significant but varying degrees) to diversionary attempts by competitors, buyers, suppliers and even employees. *Sustainability* analysis, the topic of chapter 5, concerns the scope and speed of such diversion. By identifying the threats to the sustainability of superior positions and the determinants of their intensity, it suggests ways of refining first-cut comparisons of positioning value. It also highlights the sticky factors whose continued scarcity is critical to the preservation of superior competitive positions.

The natural presumption in both positioning and sustainability analysis is that the organization will stick with the strategic option it selects initially. But the arrival of additional information over time may mandate a revision of the initial choice. Chapter 6, on *flexibility* analysis, focuses on such revision possibilities and shows that they represent an independent source of value that must be added to expected positioning-cum-sustainability value in order to rank options properly. In addition to forcing the organization to keep uncertainty in view, this sort of analysis helps set checkpoints for comparing progress with plans.

Irrespective of how carefully the analyses of positioning, sustainability and flexibility are conducted, errors may creep into them. Chapter 7, on *judgment*, discusses various ways to reduce the likelihood of both honest mistakes and deliberate distortions in the ranking of strategic options. It also points out, however, that not all error can be eliminated and that each organization therefore faces the challenge of striking the right balance between errors of commission and of omission in making its choices.

I focus, for reasons discussed earlier in this chapter, on applying this framework to the analysis of strategic choices. The examples in the chapters that follow will indicate that this style of analysis also facilitates the implementation of strategic options by forcing advance consideration of the actions that are required. The framework can be used, in addition, for purely diagnostic purposes such as the valuation of businesses. Finally, I hope that it will fulfill the broader purpose of forcing managers to think about important issues that they may have tended to ignore.

SUMMARY

Commitment complicates choice. The only practical way of coping with these complications is to focus attention on the few choices that are commitment-intensive: choices in which at least one of the feasible options involves significant sunk costs, opportunity costs, lead times or symbolism. Such commitment-intensive or strategic choices are the only ones likely to have a significant impact on the future; they are therefore the ones that deserve extra attention. The rest of this book elucidates the form that that extra attention should take.

4

→>> <<←

Positioning: Creating Value

If a man . . . make a better mousetrap than his neighbor, tho' he build his house in the woods, the world will make a beaten path to his door.

—Ralph Waldo Emerson, *Lectures*

The last chapter explained that commitment-intensive or strategic choices are choices among significantly different bundles of durable, specialized, untraded factors, and that they resist yet nevertheless require in-depth analysis. It is useful to begin such analysis by thinking through the *position* (i.e., strengths and weaknesses) each strategic option implies with respect to product market competitors. Emerson explained why more than a century ago. Suppose you are deciding whether to try to develop a new type of mousetrap. The first thing to look at is how the innovation will stack up against competing mousetraps. If the innovation is no better than them, it is unlikely to generate much value. If it does offer some sort of advantage, however, it is worth further thought.

This chapter describes the framework that has been developed in the last few decades for analyzing the positions implied by strategic options. In order to avoid having to tackle the complexities of commitment all at once, it invokes two assumptions that conveniently restrict, in the customary way, the scope of positioning analysis. The first simplifying assumption is that the value to the organization's owners of the pursuit of one commitment option as opposed to another is independent of the differential reactions of competitors, buyers, suppliers, employees and other interested parties. The second one is that the organization will persist with the course of action favored by the option it initially elects to pursue. Because of these assumptions, positioning analysis is substantively incomplete.

Fortunately, the restrictive assumptions implicit in positioning analysis, of zero differential reactions and zero revisions, can be relaxed. Chapter 5, on *sustainability* analysis, dispenses with the assumption of zero differential reactions and thereby adds a game-theoretic dimension to the decision-theoretic outlook characteristic of much of the work on positioning.[1] Chapter 6, on *flexibility* analysis, dispenses with the second restrictive assumption, of zero revisions. This generalization requires a full-blooded treatment of uncertainty and its interaction with irreversibility, informed by recent insights from informational economics.

Taken together, chapters 4 through 6 outline a coherent way of comparing the aggregate values of strategic options by overlaying considerations of sustainability and flexibility on option-by-option estimates of positioning value. This chapter is simply meant to help us get to a first-cut evaluation of such options, under restrictive yet convenient assumptions that can later be relaxed. Its conceptual fare is sandwiched between two examples. The first example, which follows immediately, should hint at the power of positioning analysis, in spite of its restrictive assumptions, to sharpen strategic choice. The second example, toward the end of the chapter, is meant as a review.

Reconsider the Launch of the Lockheed TriStar.

The best way to illustrate what positioning analysis can do for you is to apply it to a strategic choice of a sort that is widely supposed to defy careful analysis: the launch of a large new passenger jet. Newhouse (1982, p. 3) has nicely evoked the atmosphere of such choices:

> In deciding to build a new airliner, a manufacturer is literally betting the company, because the size of the investment may exceed the company's entire net worth. The remarkable scale

on which they operate induces a curiously understated, rather casual style among senior executives in this industry. Betting the company, for example, is being "sporty."

Lockheed was being rather sporty, in spring 1968, when it bet nearly three times its net worth on a three-engine wide-body jet later named the TriStar. Since the failure of its last big commerical launch, the Electra, in 1955, Lockheed had become almost entirely dependent on military sales, a condition that its top management wanted to rectify. In late 1966, when it lost the government-run competition to build the U.S. supersonic transport (SST), its chairman, Daniel Haughton, reacted by putting the SST designers to work on the wide-body.

Wide-bodies, with two passenger aisles rather than one, were made possible by the "high-bypass (power)" jet engines developed for the C-5A military transport, a project on which Lockheed was the prime airframe contractor. Boeing's 747, discussed in chapter 2, represented the first attempt to commercialize high-bypass jet engines: it used four of them. But the 747 seemed, like the 707 which had pioneered narrow-body jet technology ten years earlier, to leave a hole in the market for smaller planes powered by the same engine. There were two smaller alternatives to the four-engine 747: a three-engine design optimized for about three-quarters of its capacity, and a two-engine design optimized for about one-half. Lockheed picked the trijet rather than the twin-jet, and was quickly followed into the same market segment by McDonnell Douglas' DC-10.

By spring 1968, the pattern of early orders plus the precommitment of McDonnell Douglas to the market for large commercial aircraft had made it clear that if Lockheed pushed ahead with the TriStar, it would have to split the market with the DC-10. At this juncture, Lockheed had committed only 1% to 2% of the billion-plus dollars thought to be required for the development of the TriStar. It went ahead anyway, without ever really questioning the commercial viability of a position as a trijet duopolist rather than monopolist. By its own account, it eventually lost about $2.5 billion on the TriStar program—an average of $10 million on each plane sold until the program was terminated in 1983. More careful analysis of the costs and benefits of achieving a duopoly position in trijets might have averted these losses by suggesting that the TriStar could not possibly pay for itself off a split market.

To see how more careful analysis might have helped Lockheed, it is necessary to review the analysis that it actually undertook. According to the information I have been able to piece together, Lockheed anticipated that the total nonrecurring outlays on developing and tooling up for the TriStar would be on the order of $1 billion, and that recurring production costs would be subject to a 77% learning curve, approximating $15.5 million for the 150th TriStar and $12 million for the 300th. Based on these estimates and a price forecast of $15.5 million per plane, the (undiscounted) cumulated cash flow from the TriStar program would turn positive in the vicinity of 300 planes—a sales target Lockheed was confident of surpassing when it made its announcement.

When McDonnell Douglas announced the directly competitive DC-10 three months later, Lockheed's top managers asked themselves whether they could still sell 300 TriStars—the number had been detached from the context in which it had been derived—and came up affirmative, largely because of a sense that their plane was technically superior. Lockheed went ahead with the TriStar and was saved from bankruptcy only by the grace of the U.S. government. Where, in analytical terms, did it go astray?

Most obviously, Lockheed's analysis failed to account for its cost of capital and thereby seriously underestimated the TriStar's true break-even point. The assumption of a zero cost of capital in break-even calculations, while customary in the aircraft industry, had become dysfunctional by the time the development costs for a new plane exploded into ten figures. In 1968, high-grade, long-term corporate bonds were yielding 8% or 9%, suggesting the application of at least a 10% discount rate to the cash flows expected from the TriStar program and implying a serious threat of bankruptcy in the event of program failure. Reinhardt (1973) has calculated that at a 10% discount rate, Lockheed would have lost nearly $250 million, in present value terms, if it sold 300 planes (the undiscounted "break-even") at the price and pace it had originally forecast. The true break-even point under those assumptions appears to have been slightly over 500 planes. Raising the discount rate to 15% would have raised the break-even point to over 1,000 planes. Accounting for its cost of capital should therefore have suggested to Lockheed that even if its (optimistic) forecasts for trijet demand were fulfilled, the TriStar would have to capture nearly two-thirds of that market, rather than a bit more than a third, to pay for itself.

Could Lockheed's trijet decisively beat McDonnell Douglas'? Lockheed seems to have assumed that the superior design of the TriStar (and its Rolls-Royce engines) would assure its competitive success. It seems, for that reason, to have taken a very narrow view of benefits to buyers. The TriStar *did* have some appealing characteristics (in such respects as hydraulics, cockpit layout and the mount for the tail-engine) relative to the DC-10, but it had become clear by spring 1968 that the airlines would not pay more for one plane than for the other. Any residual design-related disadvantage for the DC-10 was more than offset by its various advantages. The reputation of McDonnell Douglas enabled the DC-10 to secure the two largest domestic carriers, United and American, as its launch customers: they had had doubts about Lockheed since the Electra debacle and simply didn't trust its British engine supplier, Rolls-Royce (which had, up to that point, been shut out of the U.S. market). They regarded McDonnell Douglas, in contrast, as the one supplier that might give Boeing a run for its money and therefore, other things being reasonably equal, the one to favor. Without United and American, there would have been no DC-10; with their orders in hand, McDonnell Douglas arguably entered the next phase of the competition stronger, not weaker, than Lockheed.

The DC-10 also managed to achieve a timing advantage over the TriStar, for reasons including its more evolutionary design and McDonnell Douglas' prior experience with large passenger jets. The potential for such an advantage was evident in the late 1960s, even before Lockheed ran into unanticipated problems with its engine supplier and its military contracts. While Lockheed was planning to work on just one version of the TriStar in the first few years of its trijet program, McDonnell Douglas was planning to develop, over roughly the same time frame, two versions of the DC-10: one that would compete head-on with the TriStar, and an extended-range version that would compete, somewhat less directly, with the 747. If both development efforts achieved technical success—and they did—the DC-10 would have a head start at winning the rest of the race. For these reasons, it wasn't at all clear, in spring 1968, that the TriStar's superior design would allow it to outsell the DC-10, i.e., (perhaps) achieve a positive net present value.

By implication, the sales volume required to make the TriStar pay for itself seemed, on the basis of Lockheed's original projections about unit margins (discounted at 10%), unlikely to be achieved. To make matters worse, the original margin projections should themselves have been revised downward to reflect competition from

Exhibit 4.1a Impact of Price* **Exhibit 4.1b** Impact of Production Rates*

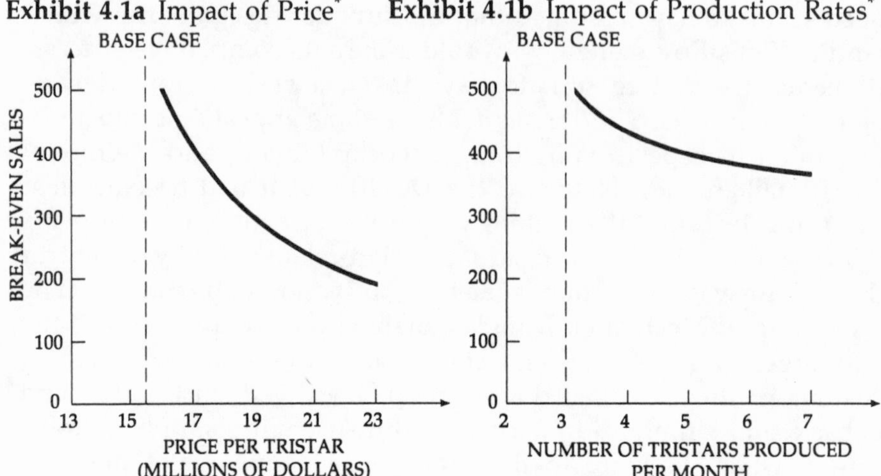

*Assumes a monthly production rate of 3 TriStars.

*Assumes a price per TriStar of $15.5 million.

SOURCE: Reinhardt (1973), pp. 832-833.

the DC-10. Competition had already forced Lockheed to cut the price of the TriStar from $15.5 million to $14.2 million. By limiting production rates and making them fluctuate, it would also raise the average level of costs. Reinhardt's (1973) analysis demonstrates that each of these margin-reducing effects could have been forecast to have a very adverse effect on the economics of the TriStar program (see Exhibits 4.1a and 4.1b). It leads him (p. 834, emphasis in original) to the conclusion that *"One may doubt that there existed in 1968 a feasible price-sales combination for the Tristar at which the program could have been expected to generate a positive net present value."*

Thus, while one can understand the desire of Lockheed's top management to reenter the commercial market, it was a poor idea to do so with a plane that could have been foreseen to lose the company a lot of money at a time when it was already overstretched. Further, even if Lockheed *was* determined to reenter the commercial market in time for the next reequipment cycle, the launch of the DC-10 should, at the very least, have forced it to reassess whether all of the twin-jet market wouldn't be better than half or less of the trijet market. Note that the European Airbus consortium later seized on the twin-jet concept and did rather well with it.

The Lockheed story illustrates the potential of positioning analysis. It also hints at some general guidelines for evaluating the competitive positions implied by different strategic options. These are systematized in the next section.

POSITIONING ANALYSIS COMPARES THE COSTS INCURRED AND THE BENEFITS DELIVERED BY STRATEGIC OPTIONS.

The modern framework for the positioning analysis of strategic choices is outlined in Exhibit 4.2. The framework's logic is straightforward. It starts with the observation that strategic choices, while hitherto viewed (in this book) from the perspective of factor deployments, have predictable implications for the level of costs incurred by the organization and the level of benefits delivered by its product(s) or service(s) to buyers. Buyers' trade-offs among competing products determine the margin-volume combinations available to the organization from each strategic option. The *positioning value* of an option is defined in terms of the most advantageous margin-volume combination it is expected to permit, i.e., in terms of the margin per unit times the number of units sold. Sometimes, as in the case of the TriStar, it is essential to trace out the margin-volume combinations over time instead of relying on timeless snapshots

Exhibit 4.2 The Framework for Positioning Analysis

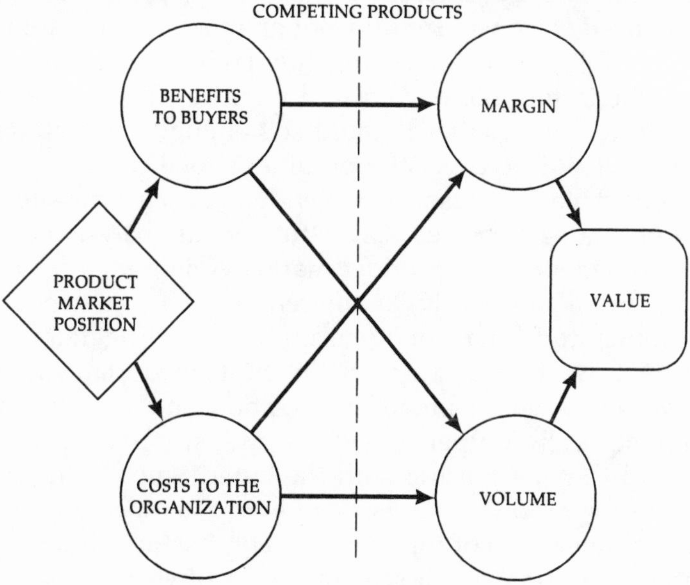

COMPETING PRODUCTS

BENEFITS TO BUYERS

MARGIN

PRODUCT MARKET POSITION

VALUE

COSTS TO THE ORGANIZATION

VOLUME

of them. Each of these elements of the received framework for positioning analysis deserves to be discussed in more detail.

The Product Market Perspective

The epigraph from Emerson hinted at the advantages of tracing the implications of commitment-intensive or strategic choices all the way through to the level at which organizations finally market their products (or services). Analysis at this level, henceforth the *product market* level, should be thought of as spanning all the functions that the organization performs *en route* to earning its daily bread. For instance, analysis at the product market level of whether to try to build a better mousetrap (or the TriStar) would pull together the implications for R&D, production and marketing instead of focusing on just one of those functions.

Adoption of the product market perspective is more than just a matter of taste or tradition. Recall, from chapter 3, that much of the difficulty of analyzing strategic choices stems from the extreme imperfections of markets for durable, specialized, generally untraded factors. These imperfections complicate direct assessments of the values of such factors. It is useful, for that reason, to exploit the long-run duality between the factor market and product market perspectives on the organization by evaluating the distinct bundles of factors implied by different options from the product market side. Lockheed, for instance, did not analyze the expenditure of a billion-plus dollars on developing the TriStar by trying to figure out what the factors thereby created might be sold for. Instead, it tried to figure out whether it could sell enough TriStars at a price that would allow it to cover the program's total costs.

The product market perspective obviously implies cross-functional analysis of strategic choices. Cross-functional analysis is essential because of evidence that product market competitors may be able to do equally well (or poorly) in different ways. For instance, Hunt's (1972) seminal study of major home appliances (refrigerators, stoves, dishwashers, washers and dryers) in the United States uncovered viable narrow- as well as broad-line positions in that industry: Maytag had historically outperformed the industry averages with the former, and General Electric with the latter. Since it does seem to be possible for product market competitors to succeed with quite different combinations of functional strengths and weaknesses, the implications of strategic choice for competitive position must be understood at a cross-functional level. Lockheed apparently forgot this point: it apparently overemphasized the TriStar's design and underemphasized considerations related to manufacturing, marketing and finance.

The product market perspective also implies that even when a strategic choice impinges on more than one product market served by the organization, its effects should be spelled out at the level of individual product markets.[2] This implication is underpinned by evidence—see Exhibit 4.3, for instance—that cross-market influences on organizational performance are, on average, an order or two of magnitude weaker than influences attributable to competitive positions in individual markets (which include both intra-industry effects and industry-level effects). To emphasize cross-market considerations at the expense of careful market-level analysis anyway is to court disaster. In launching and persisting with the TriStar, for instance, Lockheed gave too much weight to its desire to rebalance its portfolio of businesses and too little to careful analysis of the trijet market. In deference to such disasters, modern positioning theory stipulates that strategic choices should *always* be analyzed

Exhibit 4.3 Sources of Variance in Business Unit Profitability

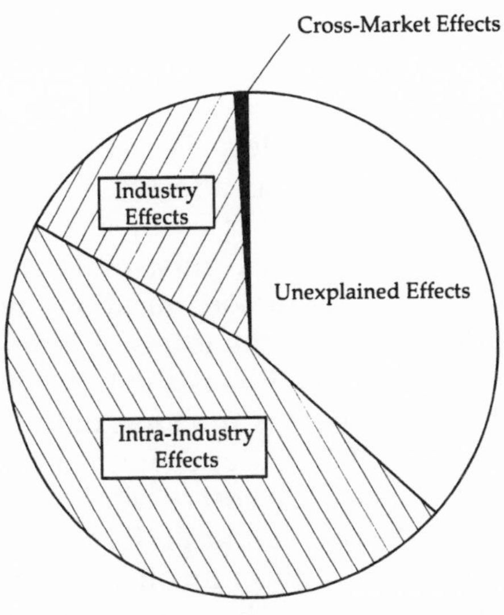

SOURCE: Rumelt (1989).

in terms of their implications for competitive positions in individual product markets.

Agreement on a product market focus does not automatically delimit product market boundaries. It is widely accepted, however, that such boundaries should be drawn broadly enough to account for substitute products that fulfill the same buyer needs.[3] In addition to comparing a new mousetrap with competing ones, for instance, one must also reckon with other devices that help control mice (e.g., the ultrasonic ones that are supposed to repel rather than eliminate the problem). This emphasis on taking substitutes into account is part of a broader purpose of the product market perspective: of forcing the organization to keep its eyes on its environment instead of on its navel.

At a procedural level, product market definition must be responsive to the organization's internal structure as well as its external environment. Internal structure, particularly the way the organization is partitioned into subunits, influences the form in which the information required for strategic analysis is most easily obtained. On occasion (e.g., if internal structure is in shambles), considerations of accuracy may outweigh considerations of ease: an extensive clean-up of the available information may then be in order. Given the expense (and delay) of setting up new channels of information for each analysis, however, extensive clean-up efforts should be the exception rather than the rule.[4]

Costs to the Organization

Modern positioning theory models the organization as mediating between suppliers and buyers. As a result, analysis of the product market implications of strategic choices must proceed on two fronts: on the supply side, the strategist must understand the levels of costs that will be incurred by the organization under different options, and on the demand side, the levels of benefits it will deliver to buyers as a result. Cost analysis is the topic of this subsection, and analysis of benefits to buyers the topic of the next one.

Comprehensiveness is the first and most obvious guideline for cost analysis. Organizations incur costs in adding or shedding factors as well as in deploying them (i.e., in performing specific functions with them). Cost behavior cannot, for that reason, be understood in terms of a single function, such as production. Instead, it must be understood broadly, across factors as well as functions.

Second, it is usually advantageous to unbundle aggregate costs into component categories. Lockheed, for instance, should have unbundled nonrecurring and recurring costs instead of mushing them together by emphasizing cumulated cash flow. There are several general reasons, in addition to what happened to Lockheed, for unbundling aggregate costs. First, the one-time costs associated with adding or shedding factors must be treated differently from the flow costs associated with performing specific functions if the two cost categories are to be added up sensibly. Second, even flow costs deserve to be unbundled if their components behave sufficiently differently. Third, unbundling forces advance consideration of how the functions associated with specific cost components will be fine-tuned to the stock of factors implied by a particular strategic option. Unbundling thereby facilitates option implementation as well as evaluation.

The TriStar case also hints at a general procedure for unbundled cost analysis: split aggregate costs into a limited number of categories expected to behave in interestingly different ways and specify a limited number of *drivers* that will affect the level of costs incurred in each category. Reconsider Reinhardt's (1973) positioning analysis of the TriStar. He first split its aggregate costs into nonrecurring and recurring categories. He then specified the cost drivers relevant to each category: the total number of TriStars sold would be the chief driver of the average level of nonrecurring costs (since total nonrecurring costs were largely fixed), and the recurring costs per unit would be driven, primarily, by the rate of output and the number of TriStars already produced. But this is all very case-specific. How, in general, should cost categories and their drivers be identified?

Common sense, backed up by systematic empirical research (Collis 1986), suggests several rules for splitting up aggregate costs. First, cost categories deserve to be broken out (instead of being lumped together) only if the factor differentials among the options being considered are likely to influence them in different ways. Second, discrete cost categories must be technically separable: there would be no sense in carrying two separate cost categories through the entire analysis if the choice about how to perform the functions subsumed by one totally determined how the functions subsumed by the other were to be performed as well. Third, individual cost categories should be large enough to exert significant influences on overall business performance. Fourth, organizational structure must also be attended to because, as discussed in the previous subsection, it determines the form in which the information required for strategic analysis is most easily obtained: data are frequently prepackaged in ways that favor a particular way of splitting up costs. Finally, generic templates such as McKinsey's business system (Bales et al. 1980) or Porter's (1985) value chain may sometimes be useful in deciding how to unbundle costs in specific instances. Note that such templates typically involve fewer than ten discrete cost categories.

If cost categories are one pillar of strategic cost analysis, cost drivers are the other. Bain (1956) initiated the systematic discussion of cost drivers by distinguishing between size-related and "absolute" (size-unrelated) ones. Porter (1985, chap. 3) has elaborated and extended Bain's classification into a menu of ten generic cost drivers: three that are broadly related to size or to the fixed costs that make size matter (economies and diseconomies of scale, learning and spillovers, and the pattern of capacity utilization), three that address various types of linkages (across the functions performed by an individual organizational subunit and across vertically and horizontally related organizational subunits), and four that can only be classified as miscellaneous (timing, policy choices, location and institutional factors). Porter makes a convincing case that the behavior of each cost category should be understood in terms of a limited number of drivers off this menu, and that the numbers added up into aggregate costs should reflect such an understanding. To return to the TriStar, Reinhardt (1973) modeled recurring and nonrecurring costs as (different) functions of just two cost drivers: scale (the rate of output) and learning (output over time).

Common sense suggests several determinants of the number and nature of cost drivers selected per cost category. Other things being equal, categories that account for a thicker slice of costs deserve more attention, i.e., treatment in terms of more cost drivers. The analysis of any particular cost category should focus on the drivers that have the biggest impact on it. Additionally, the effects of a particular cost driver require modeling only if the options being analyzed afford significantly different degrees of leverage with respect to that driver.[5] Reinhardt's cost model supports my sense that analysis of an individual cost category rarely requires more than two or three cost drivers.

Benefits to Buyers

The costs to the organization of doing one thing as opposed to another are just part of positioning analysis: differences in the benefits delivered to buyers by different strategic options must also be taken into account. Benefits actually seem to pack more of a punch: differences in the levels of benefits delivered seem to account for more of the performance variation observed among product market competitors than do differences in the levels of costs that they incur.[6] The analysis of benefits to buyers is, as a result, important for all products except a few "pure" commodities.

Benefits tend, however, to be harder to unravel than costs, for several reasons. Picturing the organization as a bundle of factors, benefits tend to depend comparatively more heavily on intangible (i.e., physically immeasurable) factors than do costs. Picturing it in terms of the functions that it performs, cost analysis can be conducted on the basis of (relatively) objective technical relationships, but benefit analysis requires assumptions about subjective buyer preferences as well as objective information about products. Finally, individual cost categories, once analyzed, can simply be added up, whereas overall product benefits may have a more complicated (i.e., nonadditive) structure. Despite these difficulties, it *is* possible to lay down some general guidelines for the analysis of benefits to buyers.

Benefit analysis should be grounded in *characteristics,* the objective attributes of products that are relevant to choice by buyers. In the TriStar case, these included attributes such as seating capacity, range, fuel efficiency, noise levels and redundancy of key subsystems. Characteristics are meant to crystallize notions about buyers' wants. They may enter buyers' benefit functions either positively or negatively. They are appropriately measured in terms of gross rather than net (of price) benefits to buyers: price should be thought of not as a characteristic, but as the gross payoff per unit afforded by serving up a particular bundle of characteristics. To flag the relevant characteristics, one must understand how the buyer actually uses the product or service. This may, on occasion, involve fairly elaborate analysis of the functions the *buyer* performs (Porter 1985, chap. 3). The example toward the end of this chapter will reinforce this point.

A thorough understanding of the buyer's consumption process usually suggests an unmanageably long list of characteristics that might matter. One of the major challenges in benefit analysis is to pare this unwieldy long list down to a short list of characteristics whose effects can be understood in appropriate detail. Lancaster's (1971, chap. 9) analysis of buyer choice among competing products suggests several rules for doing so. First, if the total contribution of a group of competing products to a particular characteristic is small in relation to the contribution from products outside the group, that characteristic can be neglected in the analysis of the small group. Second, a characteristic that is invariant over the group of competing products is analytically irrelevant. (As a corollary, if two or more characteristics are possessed by all competing products in a fixed ratio, all but one of them can be treated as irrelevant.) Third, even if competitors within the group deliver different levels of a particular characteristic, such differentials should be ignored if they fail, because of either satiation or domination, to affect buyer choice. Fourth, of the characteristics that do affect buyer choice, it is useful to focus on the ones to which it is most sensitive. By thinking along such lines, Lockheed might have been able to avoid making too much of the TriStar's design-related refinements.

Since Lancaster defined characteristics objectively, his analysis of benefits must be supplemented with subjective considerations. Porter (1985, chap. 3) has suggested thinking about the subjective component of buyer choice in terms of *signals* of benefits. Signals of benefits are distinct from characteristics in that they influence buyers' perceptions of the organization's ability to satisfy their wants rather than the organization's actual ability to do so. Porter has compiled an interesting list of such signals: reputation or image, cumulative advertising, weight or outward appearance of the product, packaging and labels, appearance and size, time in business, installed base, customer list, market share, price (where price connotes quality), parent company identity (size, financial stability, etc.) and visibility to top management of the buying firm (1985, p. 144). Lockheed slighted signaling considerations in analyzing the TriStar. While it was right to assume that the TriStar's superior design would appeal to airlines' engineering staffs, it was wrong to gloss over the fact that first-buys would largely be determined by top managers more skeptical of Lockheed than of McDonnell Douglas—the fact that objective design-related characteristics would be just one of the inputs into the trijet buying process.

Note that the objective (characteristic-related) and subjective (signal-related) approaches to benefit analysis are quite compatible with each other. The former implicitly assumes that buyers maximize net benefits to themselves, and the latter lets one probe the reasons they may not actually do so. By implication, the objective part of benefit analysis emphasizes the technology of the consumption process and the subjective part the structure of the buying process.

While the appropriate allocation of attention between the two may vary from situation to situation, it is essential to keep both in view.

Comparison with Competitors

The preceding discussion might have seemed to be headed toward the conclusion that the organization should try, in each of the product markets that it serves, to push down costs incurred and push up benefits delivered. That conclusion too closely approximates the advice to buy low and sell high, however, to be worthy of distinctive celebration. What turbocharges the framework for positioning analysis is the idea, implicit in Emerson, that competition mediates between product costs and benefits on the one hand and attainable margin-volume combinations on the other. Margin times volume is equal, of course, to (positioning) value.

To capitalize on this idea, consider the simple depiction of product market economics in Exhibit 4.4. A buyer, faced with competing products, will tend to select the one that maximizes (real or imagined) net benefits: the gross benefits from a product minus the price he or she must pay for that product. The net return available to the organization per unit of product, its *margin,* will equal the gross benefits of the product minus its costs as well as the level of net benefits it must deliver to buyers to attract them in the face of competition. Margin will, as a result, vary inversely with the intensity of competition. When the intensity of competition is low, a business can capture nearly all of the gap between product benefits

Exhibit 4.4 Product Market Economics

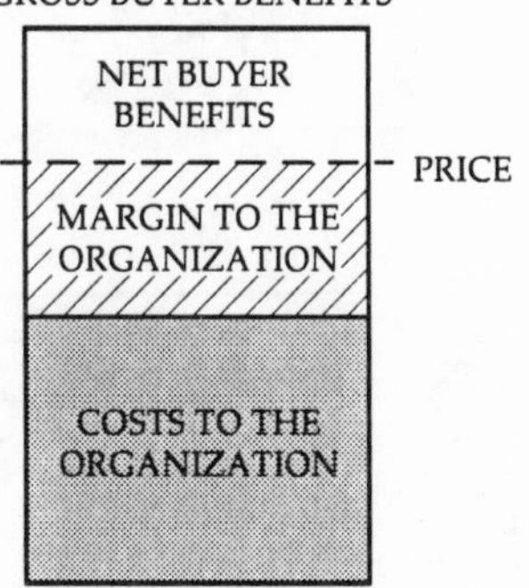

and product cost (its *efficiency*) as margin, i.e., successfully engage in value pricing. In contrast, when the intensity of competition is high, the business' margin will not be much higher than its *competitive advantage,* the extent to which the benefit-cost gap for its product exceeds the benefit-cost gaps for competitors' products. It is important to supplement considerations of efficiency with considerations of competitive advantage because even apparently minor operating differentials *vis-à-vis* product market competitors can have major implications for financial performance. Wal-Mart, for example, has historically enjoyed an operating margin advantage of about three percentage points *vis-à-vis* K Mart. This may not seem like very much but it has, in conjunction with Wal-Mart's faster growth, ensured that the market-to-book value of its common stock is more than seven times as high as K Mart's (as of the end of 1990).

Michael Porter has suggested an operational way of assessing the effects of competition along a continuum as opposed to a high-low dichotomy (see Exhibit 4.5). Porter proposes using the (possibly hypothetical) average performer in the industry as the benchmark, and relating the organization's margin to that competitor's. His 1980 book, *Competitive Strategy,* develops a systematic procedure for assessing average industry margin. The quantity that must be

Exhibit 4.5 Margin and the Intensity of Competition

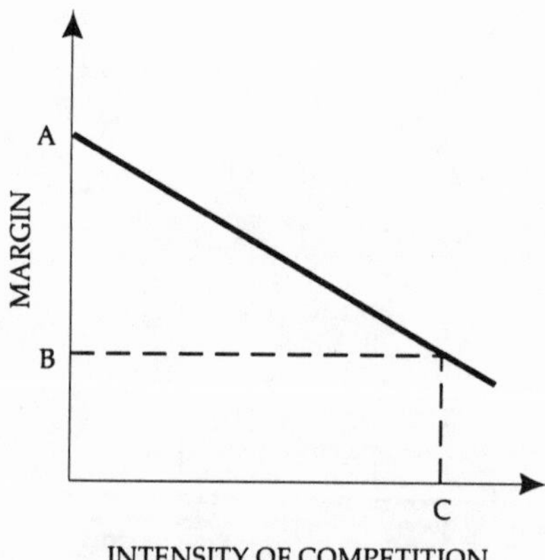

added to the industry average to estimate the margin the organization can expect for itself from a particular position is the topic of Porter's 1985 book, *Competitive Advantage.*

Using the median-ability competitor as the benchmark is, of course, just one of several possibilities. It is not equally sensible in all situations. For instance, it would have been rather roundabout for Lockheed to conceive of and compare itself with some hypothetical average competitor in trijets instead of its only direct rival, McDonnell Douglas. In the Owens-Corning Fiberglas case discussed later in this chapter, substitute technologies turned out to be the appropriate benchmarks. In the chemical sector, proposed capacity additions are often benchmarked relative to "leader" and "laggard" plants because of the importance of understanding where they will be located on the industry cost curve. In general, the (groups of) competitors that the organization expects to run up against most in either product or factor markets tend to make the best benchmarks. The precise choice of benchmark does not alter the fundamental logic of margin analysis: the margin available to the organization will equal the margin of the benchmark competitor plus the organization's competitive advantage (or minus its disadvantage) relative to that benchmark.

When buyers vary, as they usually do, in terms of either their needs, the cost of fulfilling those needs or the intensity of competition to consummate them, margin analysis must be supplemented with attention to the margin-volume trade-off that confronts the individual organization in each of its product markets. This simple idea underpins the enormous literature on segmenting the product market. Segmentation is a rough but ready way of picking up differences among (sets of) buyers along the dimensions listed above. At the level of dichotomy, the organization can either skim the cream off a relatively few, high-margin buyer segments (a *specialist* strategy) or pursue a broader target in the hopes of making up in the way of volume what it thereby loses in the way of average margin (a *generalist* strategy). More generally, the individual competitor faces, in all but perfectly competitive (and therefore strategically uninteresting) situations, a downward sloping demand curve for its product, and has some leeway in deciding how far up or down that curve to operate. On occasion, as in the case of the TriStar, such analysis may even tell the strategist that the organization cannot attain a profitable price-sales combination, i.e., a viable competitive position.

Porter (1980; 1985) has dichotomized the trade-off between margin and volume into a distinction between focus (or specialist) strategies, which are margin-oriented, and leadership (or generalist) strategies, which are more volume-oriented. The same trade-off underlies the more dynamic distinction (originally drawn by population ecologists and recently imported into business by organization theorists) between "K strategies" and "r strategies."[7] K-strategists, or specialists, are supposed to be relatively choosy about the segments they expand into (or the opportunities they pursue); r-strategists, or generalists, are supposed to be less discriminate.

While such "generic strategies" are useful heuristic devices, they do not offer a specific answer to the question of how much volume the organization should go for under the particular strategic option that it elects to pursue. The answer to that question tends, in the short run, to be governed by the amount of capacity it has precommitted to the product market in question. In the long run, capacity is variable, making matters a bit more complicated. Theory suggests, nonetheless, several conditions that favor generalist or high-volume strategies: limited heterogeneity in buyers' needs, the ability to charge different prices in different segments, significant fixed costs that do not vary with the number of buyer segments served, and the possibility of improving products by incurring additional fixed costs.[8] The opposite conditions are relatively favorable to specialist strategies.

Empirical research indicates, in addition, that the way a competitive advantage or disadvantage is channeled into value also seems to depend on its type. Cost-based advantages over competitors are primarily absorbed into extra volume, whereas benefit-based advantages tend to be taken in the form of fatter margins and, in some cases, greater volume as well (Caves and Ghemawat 1989). To illustrate, low-cost Korean competitors have adopted a low-margin/high-volume approach to the U.S. market for televisions, whereas Sony, whose TVs offer some unique benefits to buyers, concentrates on preserving its margins. Of course, this pattern is simply an average tendency; its optimality must be rechecked in each situation. As part of deciding whether to build a better mousetrap, the strategist must figure out *from the specifics of the situation* whether such a mousetrap is best priced high, attracting relatively few buyers, or lower, attracting rather more of them.

That covers the contents of Exhibit 4.2, which can now be reviewed in full. Apply the method for tracing product costs and product benefits discussed in the previous subsections to each of the commitment options available to the organization *and* to a benchmark competitor or group of competitors, with an emphasis on the dimensions along which the choice might open up significant competitive differences. Then use the logic of product market competition to identify the best margin-volume combination each option is likely to afford. This may require collapsing the buyers into a manageable number of strategic segments and building up the analysis of margin-volume combinations from the segment level (as in the Owens-Corning Fiberglas case discussed later). The identity between margin-times-volume and value will determine the positioning value of each option.

The Passage of Time

The framework for positioning analysis presented in Exhibit 4.2 is usually couched in timeless terms.[9] Lockheed's experience with the TriStar should, however, have suggested that a timeless snapshot of the margin-volume combinations afforded by a particular option may not be an adequate basis for analyzing it: that margin-volume combinations may need to be traced out over time. The strategist must worry about the passage of time whenever the time-shape of cash flows is expected to vary significantly over the options being considered. The multiyear implementation lags associated with many strategic options frequently combine with the logic of discounting to require systematic intertemporal trade-offs. At a constant annual discount rate of 15%, for instance, a dollar of value obtained with a two-year lag is presently worth 75 cents, 50 cents if obtained five years down the road, and only 25 cents if obtained ten years into the future. Effects this large cannot sensibly be ignored. As a result, the passage of time must, more often than not, be brought back into the picture.

This requirement is responsible for the appeal of the two simplifying assumptions of positioning analysis. Assumption 1, of zero differential reactions, abstracts away from action-reaction sequences to let the strategist focus on a single-player decision problem instead of a much more complicated multiplayer problem (i.e., a full-blown dynamic game among several players, each out to maximize its own net present value). Assumption 2, of zero revisions, abstracts away from expectations of changes in expectations to let the strategist focus on her or his best guess about what the passage of time holds in store. The two simplifying assumptions thereby facilitate the translation of the timeless framework for positioning into a timeful one.

Given these two assumptions, the positioning values of strategic options are sensibly estimated in terms of the *discounted cash flow* (DCF) anticipated from each of them. The anticipated period-by-period product of margin and volume figures in the numerator of DCF analysis of value streams, and the appropriate discount rate in the denominator. How considerations of time preference, inflation and risk should be distilled into a discount rate is properly the subject of finance.[10] Strategy, in contrast, is concerned with what seems to be the real locus of action: the numerator of DCF analysis. The strategic task, in other words, is to understand the evolution of the (optimal) margin-volume combination associated with each option.

The several possible methods for doing so can be ordered in terms of how demanding they are. One method, employed by Reinhardt (1973), is to analyze margin-volume combinations in detail for each and every time period (typically a calendar year). Another is to designate a particular time period as the *reference frame* that is to be analyzed in detail, and to use it as the basis for interpolations from here to there and extrapolations from there to beyond. Yet another is to collapse time into the operational categories of the short run and the long run. Finally, in a few situations (such as the one confronting Owens-Corning Fiberglas that is discussed in the next section), a focus on the timeless long run may suffice.

Note that none of these methods gets around the problem that commitments often have open-ended effects. When this is the case, the margin-volume implications of strategic choice cannot be analyzed in full (i.e., infinite) depth.[11] The only practical way of dealing with this problem is to specify an artificial *horizon,* a period beyond which the evolution of margin-times-volume will not be modeled in significant detail. In terms of the year-by-year method, value should be modeled in much greater detail before the horizon than beyond it. If one works with a reference frame, it should be set no farther out into the future than the horizon. The horizon can also be thought of as marking the boundary between the short run and the long run. It should be thought of as subsuming the latter under timeless long-run analysis.

How far out into the future should the horizon be set? While the answer must be customized to the situation, two general guidelines *can* be offered. First, the interval between the present and the horizon should be at least as long as the longest implementation lag implicit in the set of options being taken seriously. Second, the extent to which the selected interval exceeds the longest implementation lag should depend on how quickly uncertainty blurs the ability to predict differences in value from one period to the next. In situations marked by high uncertainty, set the horizon relatively close to the longest implementation lag. If, in contrast, trends in value can be predicted with some confidence beyond that time, set the horizon farther out into the future.

Judging by the way they handle commitments of physical capital, most U.S. companies employ horizons that extend no more than a decade into the future, with focal points around three, five and ten years (Pohlman, Santiago and Markel 1988). Too many of them, I suspect, do themselves a disservice by insisting on a fixed horizon for all choices subject to formal analysis, those that involve little commitment as well as those that involve a lot. For reasons discussed in the previous chapter, there should be more variability in the choice of horizon: significant commitments should be analyzed in extra depth. A shift toward the appropriate level of variability would presumably shift the average horizon for *strategic* analysis farther out into the future.

Analysis up to the horizon, if any, should account for investment or disinvestment differentials (e.g., the expected costs of developing a better mousetrap) as well as variations in the operating cash flows associated with different options, and should also reckon with trends, broadly defined. One obvious trend, which is the basis of the extensive literature on the product life cycle, concerns the growth (or shrinkage) rate of the served market. Growth, even if anticipated, tends to have a positive effect on the margins as well as volumes of product market competitors (Bradburd and Caves 1982). Once again, however, this is a broad empirical pattern whose validity must be assessed for the situation at hand rather than simply assumed. There are many trends other than market growth that may also repay attention: the evolution of buyer needs, the general rate of process and product innovation, shifts in competitive scale, input costs and exchange rates, developments in linked industries and in government policy, and so forth (Porter 1980, chap. 8). Because of the simplifying assumptions that underlie positioning analysis, developments along each relevant dimension can be treated as exogenous. One best guess about each relevant trend will suffice for the analysis of *all* strategic options.

The evolution of margin and volume at or beyond the horizon has to be handled in cruder ways because uncertainties take over as one tries to forecast farther and farther out into the future. As a result, cycles and one-time discontinuities that far out are usually ignored, and only the simplest, most significant trends taken into account. That does not mean, however, that the deep future is irrelevant to the analysis: commitment-intensive choices are important precisely because of their long-run implications. While the estimates of margin and (rate of growth of) volume that are the key parameters in the long run should, in the first instance, be derived from the analysis of product market competition, they need to be supplemented with considerations of sustainability and flexibility, as discussed in chapters 5 and 6.

Positioning analysis can usefully be reillustrated.

An additional example of positioning analysis may be useful in several respects: to squelch suggestions that careful analysis always leads to paralysis, to highlight a somewhat different set of analytical points from the TriStar example and just to make the last section's message more vivid. Consider, for all these reasons, the choice among membrane technologies that Owens-Corning Fiberglas (OCF) was faced with in the U.S. commercial roofing membrane market in 1980.[12]

The sorts of commercial roofing membranes sold in the United States had changed significantly since the early 1970s (see Exhibit 4.6). Glass built-up roofing (BUR) membranes had seized a significant share of the market from the organic and asbestos BUR membranes that had overwhelmingly dominated it in the past, and single-ply systems (SPS) of varying chemical composition had also gained a foothold.[13] OCF had pioneered glass BUR membranes and still dominated that category with its Perma Ply-R product. Perma Ply-R continued to register volume gains in 1980, but its margin had started to come under pressure. Instead of ignoring the problem in the hope that it would go away or focusing on the most direct threat (in this instance, on the weaker-but-cheaper mats that had been introduced by glass BUR competitors), OCF recognized that the threat from substitutes was real, and that if it waited for single-ply membranes to penetrate further before choosing how to act, it might lose its room for maneuver. It had to try to assess the market

Exhibit 4.6 Market Shares of Commercial Roofing Membranes

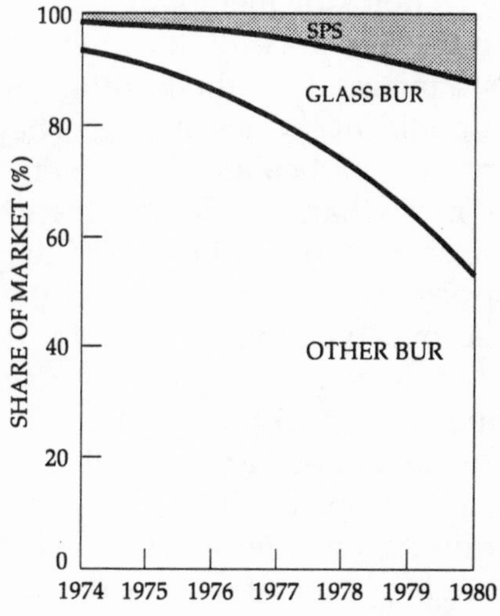

potentials for different types of BUR and single-ply membranes ahead of time. This involved comparing the long-run competitive positions of these products on the basis of what was known about them in 1980.

On the cost-analytic front, membrane type was, by assumption, the single most important cost driver to be examined. The prices of single-ply membranes and estimates of the margins earned on them by competitors suggested that they cost about twice as much per square foot of roof covered as did BUR membranes. By implication, the SPS-to-BUR threat, if any, came from the benefit side rather than the cost side. OCF focused, therefore, on understanding benefits delivered to buyers by competing membrane types in much greater depth than the costs incurred in their manufacture. This required thinking through how membranes were bought and used.

Although the expense of roofing was ultimately borne by building owners, the analysis focused on roofing contractors, who actually installed roofs, as the *real* buyers: they accounted for the choice of product type in the majority of cases. There were many thousands of roofing contractors in the United States in 1980. Materials accounted for the bulk of their costs. According to a survey by their trade association, roofing contractors got most of their business by submitting the lowest bid, and most of them had already tried single-ply membranes. As all this might indicate, roofing contractors were very cost-sensitive: the characteristic that they most wished to minimize in their choice of membrane type was the total cost of installing the roof. The price of the membrane was just one element of the costs incurred by them: other materials and labor also accounted for significant chunks of costs. They would be willing to pay a dollar more for a particular type of membrane if it lowered their other costs by more than a dollar. So the extra benefits delivered, in terms of the characteristic of cost-effectiveness, by one type of membrane as opposed to another equaled the membrane-unrelated costs for the second type minus those for the first.

It now became clear why some buyers were willing to purchase single-ply membranes at a price of about $60 per 100 square feet rather than the three layers of Perma Ply-R required to cover the equivalent area at a total expenditure of about $15. For a large, ballastable roof requiring an intermediate level of insulation, for example, use of a single-ply membrane might save the roofing contractor $27 in insulation costs (because the most cost-effective type of insulation on the market, bead board, was incompatible with the hot asphalt in BUR sandwiches), about $10 in the costs of other materials, primarily asphalt, and about $10 in labor costs.

The example should have suggested that the relative benefits delivered by different types of membrane depended on the parameters of the roof to be laid. Not all roofs were insulated; on the ones that weren't, BUR looked rather more competitive. The same was true for roofs on buildings that could not bear the load of ballast: single-ply membranes had to be attached to such roofs with nails or adhesive, which was a much more time-consuming process than simply holding them in place with ballast.[14] Roof size was a factor as well because it tended to be inversely related to the amount of flashing that had to be installed to seal the roof perimeter and "penetrations" such as chimneys. The flashing for BUR systems was relatively expensive and costly to install, implying a comparative advantage for them in large, less flashing-intensive applications. To take account of such systematic variations, OCF segmented the commercial roofing market along the dimensions of insulation requirements, ballastability, and roof size to yield 18 (3 × 2 × 3) segments. It focused the rest of its analysis on trying to understand the likely long-run competitive positions of the different types of membranes at the level of individual segments.

The obvious place to start was by identifying the lowest installed-cost roofing system in each segment in 1980. The results of this

Exhibit 4.7 Lowest Installed-Cost Roofing System by Segment*

	BALLAST ALLOWED			NO BALLAST ALLOWED		
	SMALL ROOF	MEDIUM ROOF	LARGE ROOF	SMALL ROOF	MEDIUM ROOF	LARGE ROOF
MAXIMAL INSULATION	MB	EPDM	EPDM	MB	BUR	BUR
SOME INSULATION	MB	EPDM	EPDM	MB	BUR	BUR
MINIMAL INSULATION	MB	BUR	BUR	MB	BUR	BUR

*Membranes factored in at 1980 market prices.

exercise, reported in Exhibit 4.7, merit some discussion. The only BUR systems that appeared to be competitive in such terms, glass-based ones like OCF's, were favored by minimal insulation requirements and lack of ballastability, and on relatively large roofs. Ethylene propylene diene monomer (EPDM), the type of single-ply membrane that had achieved the largest share by 1980 (about 7%), looked competitive on relatively large roofs that required insulation and could be ballasted. The most surprising result, however, was that another type of single-ply membrane that held only 2% of the overall market in 1980, modified bitumen (MB), looked low cost in about 32% of the market—on small roofs—because of its extremely cheap flashing. The corresponding market potential figure for glass BUR was 40%, and for EPDM 28%.

Taken at face value, these market potential numbers might have suggested that the prospects for glass BUR weren't that bad: that it might even pick up a few percentage points of market share since its 1980 share stood at "only" 36%. To have stopped with these numbers, however, would have been to confuse prices (outcomes) with the thing underlying them that is of real interest, namely, competitive position. The procedure for positioning analysis discussed in the last section depends on comparisons of costs incurred and benefits delivered by competitors instead of prices charged. The distinction matters in the OCF case because it was clear in 1980 that the EPDM pricing structure was about to collapse: Carlisle, the pioneer, had so far managed to skim the market with prices that had 50% margins built into them, but huge amounts of EPDM capacity were in the process of being added by other companies, particularly other tire manufacturers. What was required in order to figure out competitive position—which type of membrane could ultimately undersell all the rest in which segment—was a comparison of total installed costs that accounted for membranes not at market prices (as in Exhibit 4.7) but at costs to manufacturers. Redoing the installed cost analysis on this basis, segment by segment, and adding up the results exposed the true dimensions of the threat to glass BUR, which had much less to play with in the way of initial margin: its market potential fell to 15%, with EPDM and modified bitumen splitting the remainder.

Even though EPDM and MB came out even on this "market potential at cost" comparison, they did not on several others. Consider, first, competition among different types of membranes. Modified bitumen, where it was low cost, had a bigger advantage over the next lowest-cost system than EPDM did in the segments where *it* was low cost in 1980. This advantage could be expected to grow over time and modified bitumen's market potential to expand, because its costs were forecast to inflate relatively slowly.[15] Consideration of competition *within* membrane types also inclined OCF toward MB. Modified bitumen had attracted fewer, less cutthroat competitors than EPDM. Even if competition among MB producers reduced their average margin to zero, OCF felt that it could achieve lower costs than them because the modified bitumen membrane used some glass mat as a reinforcement, and OCF knew how to make stronger glass mat than anyone else. EPDM, in contrast, did not offer OCF the prospect of any advantage.

This analysis led directly to action. OCF entered the modified bitumen market by forming a strategic alliance with an earlier entrant, Derbigum, which was partly owned by 50 of the largest roofing contractors in the United States, and later consolidated its entry by acquiring Derbigum. It immediately began to invest R&D dollars in the development of a more cost-effective MB membrane, and managed to introduce one in 1984. It also began work on, and eventually introduced, an insulation material designed to complement MB better than any other insulation on the market. This strategic thrust seems to have worked out rather well: OCF has become the leader in MB membranes which have, in turn, become the single largest element of the commercial roofing market and continue to enjoy healthier margins than membranes under more pressure from substitutes. Note, in particular, the way in which OCF's choice about the position that it would pursue guided its subordinate choices. It is in this indirect but important sense that considerations of positioning can help with the implementation of strategic options as well as with their selection.

To wrap up this discussion, compare the OCF story with the Lockheed story. One of the two obviously handled the choice confronting it more adroitly than the other. There is another, more interesting difference as well. Note how *effective* positioning analysis can vary considerably, to external appearances, from one situation to the next. What is important in positioning analysis is not its form, which should probably be customized to the choice being considered, but its logic, which was discussed in the last section.

Positioning analysis is an incomplete basis for strategic choice.

Positioning analysis has come a long way since Emerson orginally proposed that the choice between building and not building a new type of mousetrap be based on an assessment of whether it would offer an advantage *vis-à-vis* competing mousetraps. The modern framework for positioning analysis focuses on the competitive positions of businesses instead of products. It is much more specific than Emerson ever was about how to assess competitive position. It recognizes that the benefits afforded by a superior competitive position must be weighed against the costs of achieving it. Stretched out over time, it can also account for exogenous trends, such as the exogenous rate of improvement of competing mousetraps.

This progress notwithstanding, positioning analysis is an incomplete basis for strategic choice. In regard to the choice about whether to build a new type of mousetrap, for example, it misses out on two key considerations. First, new types of mousetraps that *have* succeeded in the marketplace (e.g., spring traps, repeating traps and glueboards) have not appreciably enriched their respective innovators, largely because of their attractions for imitators as well as mice. Second, to focus on the prospects for success of a new type of mousetrap would be to focus on the tip of the iceberg because the overwhelming majority of attempts at product innovation do not even make it as far as market testing.

Both sorts of omissions can be restated more generally. First, positioning analysis glosses over endogenous reactions (e.g., imitation of new types of mousetraps that prove to be breakthroughs): it tends to assume away differences in the reactions of competitors and other interested and influential parties to the organization's choice of one strategic option (intended long-run position) as opposed to another. Second, it fails to account for the way in which the receipt of new information may induce the organization to revise its course of action (e.g., terminate a mousetrap development program that is proving to be a bad idea): it assumes that the organization will persist, without further recourse, with the course of action favored by the option it initially elects to pursue. These omissions are rectified, respectively, in the chapters on *sustainability* and *flexibility* that follow. What needs to be noted here is that positioning analysis should be treated as the analytical starting point rather than the stopping point.

Summary

Positioning analysis involves a first-cut evaluation of commitment options. It capitalizes on the insight that commitments affect competitive positions in product markets: considerations of product market competition can therefore be pressed into service to assess the (positioning) values of commitment options. Positioning analysis does, however, abstract away from reactions to the organization's choice among its commitment options, and from the ease with which the selected option can be revised. While these assumptions are convenient, comprehensiveness demands that they be relaxed.

5

Sustainability: Claiming Value

> Every situation bears the seed of its own reversal. This is the law of nemesis: Nothing good lasts indefinitely, because others will want to share it.
>
> —David S. Landes, *Revolution in Time*

The last chapter suggested evaluating strategic options in terms of their implications for the organization's position(s) in the product market(s) that it serves. Such positioning analysis represents the analytical point of departure rather than the end of the journey. The next analytical step is to recognize that valuable product market positions invite responses by nonowners—competitors, buyers, suppliers and even employees—that tend to shrink the value passed through to the organization's owners. *Sustainability* analysis addresses the scope and speed of such shrinkage. It is meant to be overlaid on assessments of positioning value.

SUSTAINABILITY ANALYSIS IS VERY IMPORTANT.

Managers seem to underestimate the importance of sustainability analysis.[1] For some evidence on this point, consider the guessing game described next. I tracked the margins (return on investment, or ROI) reported over a ten-year period, from 1971 to 1980, by the

692 business units in the PIMS database for which such data were available.[2] I split this sample into two equally sized groups based on 1971 ROI and then, keeping businesses in the groups in which they started out, I tracked the group averages through 1980. The (initially) top group's ROI in 1971 was 39% and the bottom group's 3%. It is safe to say that the businesses in the top group started out with generally superior positions, and those in the bottom group with generally inferior ones. What do you think happened to the 36-point spread between them by 1980?

Managers confronted with this question tend to guess that the initial ROI spread between the two groups shrank by one-third to one-half over the ten-year period. Exhibit 5.1 indicates that the correct answer is greater than nine-tenths. By implication, managers understand the law of nemesis but seem to come up short in assessing the scope and speed of its operation.

Having said that, I hasten to steer the reader away from the conclusion that sustainability tends to be so close to zero that it is practically irrelevant. First, even if initially superior margins are expected to converge on the average level by the tenth year, the degree to which they can be sustained in the interim is surely of interest. The shaded area in Exhibit 5.1 indicates its importance to the average business in the top half of the PIMS sample. Second, convergence actually *wasn't* complete by the tenth year for the sam-

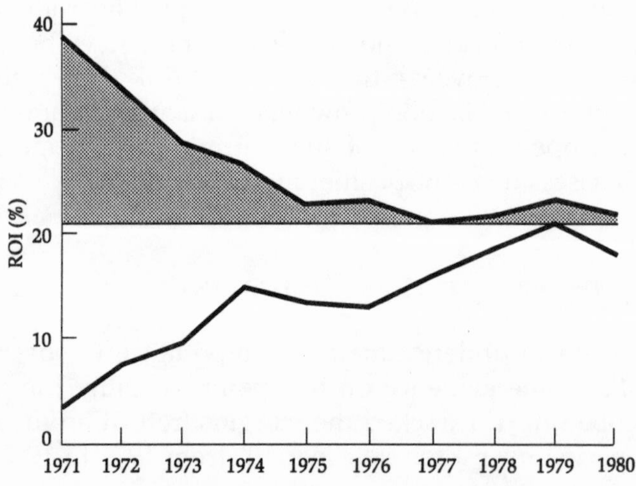

ple: the (initially) top group's average ROI was 21.5% in 1980, and the bottom group's 18.0%. A long-run spread of three-and-a-half percentage points is nothing to sneer at.[3] Third, the convergence of margins overstates the convergence of what is really of interest, margin-times-volume (value). A business earning a 39% ROI, the average for the top group in 1971, is unlikely to insist that all new investments deliver such a high rate of return, and likely to be unwise if it did.

If, in spite of these assurances, you are still taken aback by the extent to which the group averages converged, remind yourself that they mask tremendous variation. Wal-Mart is a particularly inspiring stand-out: it has ranked in the top percentile of all (but the smallest) U.S. corporations in terms of *both* profitability and growth for close to two decades now. Nearly thirty years have passed, in fact, since Mr. Sam Walton spotted the sustainability-related advantages of being the first to open a discount store in a town large enough to support one such store but not two. The analysis in this chapter systematizes the sorts of considerations that led Wal-Mart to buck the conventional wisdom and averages.

THE SUSTAINABILITY OF SUPERIOR PRODUCT MARKET POSITIONS HINGES ON COMMITMENTS TO STICKY FACTORS.

What determines the extent to which a superior product market position is likely to prove sustainable over time? That question must be answered from a factor market rather than a product market perspective. The reasons have already been discussed in chapter 2. In the absence of the factor market imperfections implied by commitment to sticky (durable, specialized, untraded) factors, the potential for frictionless entry and exit would push profits down (or up) to zero in the twinkling of an eye, regardless of initial positions. The imperfections implied by factor stickiness are therefore necessary for sustainability.

Commitment to sticky factors is not, however, sufficient for sustainability. Exhibit 5.2 outlines the two other conditions that must also be fulfilled for superior product market positions to yield sustained positive profits. First, the sticky factors that underpin them must continue to be *scarce*. Second, the owners of the organization must be able to *appropriate* some of the scarcity value that accrues to such factors. Each of these conditions deserves elaboration.

Exhibit 5.2 Conditions for Sustainability

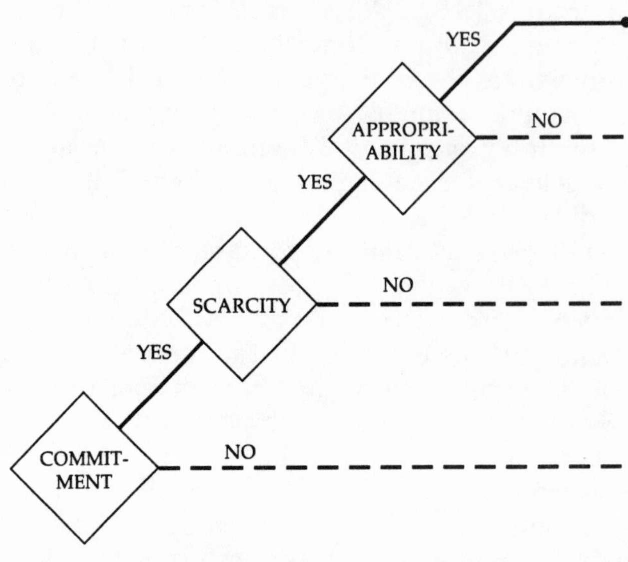

The importance of scarcity in this context can be highlighted with the air *versus* diamond example beloved by economists. Why is the air in your lungs worth less, at market prices, than the gemstone that may be on your finger? Part of the reason is that less cost is incurred in transforming the air in the atmosphere into something that you are willing to breathe than in transforming a diamond in the rough into something that you are willing to wear. But this cost differential is not the only element of the difference in prices. Differential scarcity also takes a hand. Breathable air is available in such abundant quantities that it has virtually no scarcity value in most locations. Gem-quality diamonds are clearly much scarcer. The implied difference in scarcity values accounts for most of the difference in the prices that air and diamonds can command.

The scarcity of sticky factors depends on the relation between their supply and the demand, derived from the product market side, for their services. Sustainable (positive) scarcity value requires excess demand; excess supply, in contrast, can lead to sustained losses. To test whether a strategic option offers sustainable scarcity value, it is useful to ask two kinds of questions. The first question is why excess demand won't induce competitors, actual or potential, to add to the supply of the sticky factor(s) supposed to be scarce: this is the threat of *imitation*. The second question is whether competitors, even if they are unable to attack scarcity value directly, won't be able to find a way around it: this is the threat of (factor) *substitution*.

The third condition for sustainability listed in Exhibit 5.2, appropriability, is of distinct interest because even when the factors stuck to the organization afford it scarcity value, the ability of its owners to pocket that value cannot be taken for granted. Nonowners out to further their own interests may be able to siphon off some of that value: this is the threat of *holdup*. They, particularly employees, may also squander some of it: this is the threat of *slack*. In other words, holdup threatens to divert scarcity value and slack to dissipate it.

In summary, owners who would appropriate scarcity value must contend with the law of nemesis, which threatens both the scarcity value of the organization's bundle of sticky factors and the fraction of that value the owners can expect to appropriate. More specifically, scarcity value is threatened by imitation and substitution, and appropriability by holdup and slack. These threats to sustainability have two things in common: the intensity of each tends to increase with the amount of (positioning) value generated, and each tends to take time to make its effects felt. They will be elaborated on one at a time, beginning with threats external to the organization and working in.

Imitation is a direct threat to the scarcity value of sticky factors.

Imitation threatens the scarcity value of sticky factors by expanding their supply or, when that supply is relatively fixed, by bidding up their cost. Classical economics tells us that imitation may, at the margin, shrivel scarcity value to zero. Informational and motivational considerations suggest that imitation may proceed even farther. Informational problems that induce this disturbing possibility include lags in observing competitors' commitments, correlated expectations about demand and adverse selection of the sort exemplified by the winner's curse (which is discussed in chapter 7). Excessive imitation can also be motivated by the managerial preference for expansion over contraction, compensation schemes based on performance relative to competitors and envy.

According to the cross-sectional evidence, imitation is endemic. In industries in which capacity is the most important sticky factor, an addition by one player usually triggers additions by others aimed at preserving their capacity shares. Attempts to build one's customer base tend to induce attempts by competitors to defend or develop their own: case studies such as the one presented later in this section suggest that maneuvers and countermaneuvers along this dimension often cancel out. Attempts at product differentiation based on R&D as opposed to marketing are vulnerable on several counts: competitors secure detailed information on the bulk of new products within a year of their development, patenting usually fails to deter imitation, and imitation tends to cost a third less than innovation and to be a third quicker. Process innovations do not seem to be significantly less imitable than product innovations.[4]

The most obvious way of analyzing the threat of imitation (as well as the other threats to sustainability) is to figure out which players will be most affected by the organization's strategic choice, assess their likely responses and, to the extent that those responses appear threatening, think about how they can be thwarted or blunted. But while this sort of analysis is sanctified by theory, it requires extensive information about all the competitors, actual and potential, that might respond differently to the organization's choice of one option as opposed to another.[5] It is most tractable, as a result, when response profiles need to be assembled for just one or two competitors.

When the number of competitors to be considered is larger, or when the analysis focuses on the long run, it makes more sense to look for impediments to imitation (under the assumption, implied by the law of nemesis, that imitation will occur if it is feasible) than to construct detailed response profiles. Since such impediments usually rest on precommitments to sticky factors, I will refer to them as *early-mover advantages.* There seem to be five principal forms of early-mover advantages.[6]

Private Information. One possible reason for moving early is better information. To the extent that this information can be kept private—to the extent that it is costly for would-be imitators to tap into it—imitation will be inhibited. Privacy is most likely to obtain when information is tacit rather than specifiable (i.e., doesn't lend itself to blueprinting), when it is vested in relatively few parties and when those parties are locked into long-term relationships with the early mover.

Size Economies. Size economies refer to the (possible) advantages of being large. They come in three different varieties: *scale economies,* which are the advantages of being large in a particular business at a particular point in time; *learning economies,* which are the advantages of being large in a particular business over time; and *scope economies,* which are the advantages of being large across interrelated businesses. If there *are* size economies, the early mover may be able to deter imitation by committing itself to exploiting them. That possibility depends on the would-be imitator's fear that if it tried to match the early mover's size, supply might exceed demand by enough to make it rue the effort.

Enforceable Contracts/Relationships. Early movers may be able to enter contracts or establish relationships on better terms than those available to late movers. When such arrangements are enforceable, competitors may desist from imitation on the grounds that even if it "succeeded," it would leave them at too much of a disadvantage compared to the early mover to be worthwhile. Enforceability may derive either from third-party enforcement or from self-enforcement. Examples of the former are provided by property rights and other formally specified contracts that are enforceable in court. Examples of the latter include relationships that haven't been formalized to that extent but are nevertheless expected to be sustained by buyer/supplier switching costs, risk aversion or inertia. Note that relationships with intermediaries, such as distribution channels, can also have these characteristics.

Threats of Retaliation. There are a number of reasons, including the asymmetries cited above, why early movers may be able to deter imitation by threatening massive retaliation. Talk of retaliation is, however, cheap. To be credible, it must be backed up by both the ability and the willingness to retaliate. Retaliatory moves that satisfy both conditions may either be directly profitable or reflect the early mover's demonstrated willingness to be tough with interlopers in spite of the immediate losses to itself.

Response Lags. Even if information isn't impacted, size isn't a source of economies, contracts/relationships aren't enforceable, and retaliation isn't credible, imitation usually requires a minimum length of time. From the early mover's perspective, this can be described as a response lag. Response lags are the sum of *observation lags* and *implementation lags.* Although such lags do not, by themselves, deter imitation, they obviously defer its impact.

This discussion of early-mover advantages should not, however, be misread to imply that organizations should *always* commit as early as possible. While moving early may reduce the threat of imitation, it may also involve extra cost or risk. As a result, the only sensible conclusion about early versus late timing is the one drawn long ago by Alfred P. Sloan: If you are late, you have to be better.

The threat of imitation and the impediments to it can be illustrated with a case, that of the U.S. cigarette industry between the early 1950s and the late 1960s. The U.S. cigarette market had historically consisted of two nonfiltered segments, each of which had been dominated since its inception, more or less, by one brand. In the early 1950s, however, health concerns shook up the status quo by triggering a shift to filtered cigarettes, which came to account for over 80% of the market within two decades. The experience in the nonfiltered segments had suggested the value of securing dominant positions in the filtered segments that were emerging. The response of each of the six major cigarette companies was to launch new (or extended) filtered brands with heavy advertising support aimed at establishing them as top sellers within their respective segments.

As a result, the numbers of cigarette brands exploded between the early 1950s and the late 1960s. By 1967, more than 80 total varieties, distinguished by size, filtering, mentholation, and packaging, were available (up from 18 varieties in 1951). Advertising also soared: the industry's advertising-to-sales ratio jumped from 3.8% to 8.7%, reflecting a fivefold increase in dollar expenditures that was more or less evenly distributed among the big six. These hikes, which can be regarded as imitative from the standpoint of individual producers, began to take a heavy financial toll. The investment bank of Smith Barney, for instance, publicly reckoned that the $225 million dollars the cigarette companies spent on TV and radio advertising in 1968 would have translated into that much extra operating income if such advertising had been halted. In addition, a halt would have forced federally subsidized antismoking ads (broadcast in a 1-to-3 proportion to prosmoking ads) from the airwaves, shoring up long-run demand. The profits from attempting to build up customer bases hadn't simply sunk to zero by the late 1960s; they had fallen below that level.

Although the cigarette companies understood all this, they maintained their nominal advertising levels over the 1968 to 1970 period and further increased product variety. In the terminology of game theory, they were stuck in a prisoners' dilemma and could not, acting on their own, effect jointly beneficial cuts in brand introduction rates or advertising levels, or at least not large ones. They were delivered from this stalemate in 1971 by a federal ban on the broadcast advertising of cigarettes. The cigarette industry had not been averse to such a ban. In fact, it had at one point suggested accelerating its implementation. By all accounts, it now sighed with relief that this hazard to its financial health had been removed. Without governmental intervention, the spiral of imitation could have led to long-run financial losses, not just relatively short-lived ones.

The losses that marketing mania inflicted on the cigarette industry in general mask some individual successes: some of the new filtered brands did succeed at establishing dominant, apparently inimitable positions. Such inimitability seemed to rest, for the most part, on early-mover advantages. The evidence is summarized in Exhibit 5.3, which reveals that in four of the five segments that the filtered submarket split into through 1970, there was a perfect correlation between a "top three" brand's order of entry into its particular segment and its rank (in market share terms) within the top three. The odds are less than 1 in 250 that this observed association between order of entry and market share rank could have been generated by a purely random process involving no early-mover advantages. The advantages that seem to have been the most important in this particular case include scale economies in brand marketing, self-enforcing relationships with customers based on brand loyalty, re-

Exhibit 5.3 Top Three Brands by Filter Segment

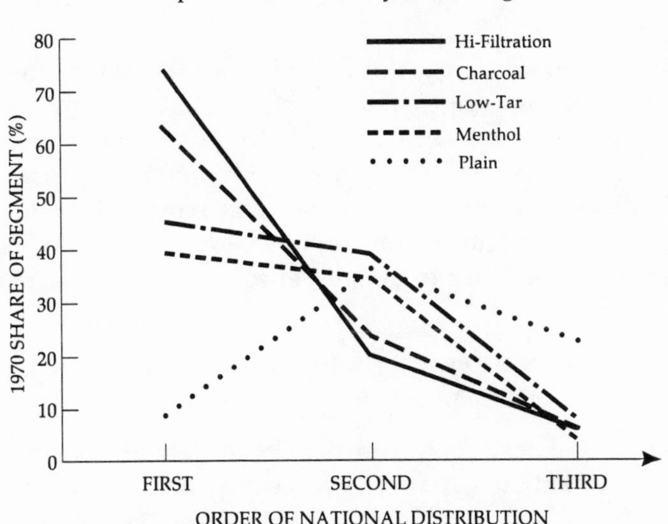

sponse lags in introducing imitative brands to compete with pioneering ones in newly identified segments and credible threats of retaliation by the pioneers. These advantages clearly cascaded in allowing some early brands to sustain their scarcity value.

The experience of the cigarette industry also reminds us, however, that moving early is no panacea. This can most clearly be seen in plain filters, the largest of the five filtered segments that emerged and the only one that did not exhibit a perfect correlation between the top three brands' market share ranks (in 1970) and their order of entry. Viceroy, a Brown and Williamson brand, was the first to achieve substantial sales in this segment. But in 1955, it was overtaken by the second-mover, R. J. Reynolds' Winston brand, which had successfully emphasized taste as well as filtration. By the end of the decade, Viceroy had also been overtaken by the third-mover, Philip Morris' Marlboro brand.

Marlboro is the brand to focus on, because it eventually overtook Winston as well as Viceroy and is now the world's single most profitable brand of nondurable consumer good. Originally targeted at female smokers, Marlboro was repositioned in 1955 with a new image and a new package. Its revised image, of a cowboy, was to become the most successful cliché in cigarette advertising. Its revised package, a crush-proof, tear-strippable, flip-top that could fit into a regular vending machine, also embodied several innovations. The Marlboro brand succeeded not because it followed some kind of mechanical timing rule (the third-mover in a specific cigarette segment isn't usually expected to do exceptionally well) but because in the minds of many smokers, its new image and package were inimitable.

In summary, brand competition in the cigarette industry reinforces the three principal messages of this section. First, the imitative addition of sticky factors is a serious threat to the sustainability of their scarcity value. Second, impediments to imitation rest on precommitments to sticky factors. Third, while it is natural to think about fruitful precommitments as early-mover advantages, an emphasis on always moving earlier than competitors would be misplaced.

Substitution is an indirect threat to the scarcity value of sticky factors.

The scarcity value of sticky factors may be threatened by substitution as well as by imitation: capacity in place may be displaced by newer and better capacity, customer preferences changed in ways that erode established customer bases and existing know-how improved on. The conceptual distinction between imitation and substitution as threats to scarcity value is that the former increases the supply of sticky factors while the latter effectively depresses the demand for them. Of course, this conceptual distinction is often less clear-cut in practice. For example, one could argue on and on about whether the later-but-better Marlboro brand imitated Viceroy and Winston in regular filters or substituted away from them. By implication, pure imitation and pure substitution should be regarded as the two ends of a spectrum of threats to scarcity value rather than as completely separate categories.

Despite this blurring at the boundaries, there are two respects in which substitution is less direct a threat to scarcity value than is imitation. First, substitution threats are less likely to be confined to direct competitors. Second, successful substitution involves finding a way around scarcity, not carrying out a direct attack on it. Such indirectness does not, however, take the sting out of substitution. In fact, some strategists have argued that substitution poses a more powerful threat to scarcity value than does imitation because indirect competition is more likely to be overlooked than direct competition, and harder to respond to once it is recognized. According to Porter (1985, p. 514), for instance, "The cardinal rule in offensive strategy is not to attack [the leader] head-on with an imitative strategy, regardless of the challenger's resources or staying power." Substitution is the approach Porter goes on to recommend for challengers who would attack the leader's early-mover advantages.

Substitution threats depend on environmental changes that create enough of a mismatch between precommitted factors and market opportunities to override early-mover advantages. While such changes can take a variety of forms, changes in technology, in demand and in the availability or prices of inputs seem, in that order, to be the most significant gateways to successful substitution. Note the implication that substitution threats are likely to be most frequent in technology-intensive, fashion-intensive and other *creative* industries in which the salient sticky factors have short half-lives, i.e., are obsolesced relatively rapidly. The computer industry highlights this threat: several participants do not even entertain ideas for fundamental product innovation unless they promise at least a tenfold improvement over the products on the market for which they are supposed to substitute. A product embodying a two- or threefold improvement in performance would probably be obsolete by the time it was introduced.

Organizations can sometimes thwart substitution threats through extra investment aimed at either defending the scarcity value of precommitted factors or replacing them in a manner responsive to environmental changes. *Renewal* of this sort has been much applauded of late. What its advocates tend to gloss over is that while relentless investment may increase earnings, it will not add value unless it is cost-effective. The threat of substitution (or of imitation) is neither immediate nor automatic, and deflecting it can be very costly. Under at least some circumstances, therefore, it must make sense to harvest rather than renew, to take the money and run. Corroboration comes from Caves, Fortunato, and Ghemawat's (1984) research on 42 "trusts" that dominated U.S. manufacturing at the turn of the century. The initial market shares of these trusts, which had been created through horizontal merger, averaged 69% and seemed substantially in excess of the levels required for them to operate efficiently. Over the next 24 years, these market shares declined significantly to an average of 45%. Their joint evolution with profit rates can be explained in terms of the optimal harvesting pattern implied by economic theory, suggesting that the trusts maximized their respective values by gradually yielding share instead of defending it against all comers.

For a contemporary example, consider the pattern of technological competition in the private branch exchange (PBX) industry. PBXs are switches located on customer premises to concentrate phone calls to central exchanges. Exhibit 5.4 summarizes their evolution through the early 1980s.[7] The first automated switch of this sort was patented in 1891 by Almon Strowger, a Kansas City undertaker, who is alleged to have been convinced that when customers tried to reach him, an operator rerouted their calls to her (the operator's)

Exhibit 5.4 The Evolution of PBX Technology

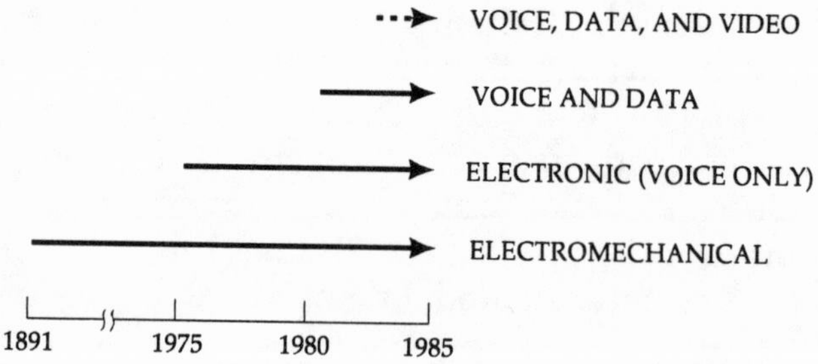

VOICE, DATA, AND VIDEO

VOICE AND DATA

ELECTRONIC (VOICE ONLY)

ELECTROMECHANICAL

1891 1975 1980 1985

husband's funeral parlor. Strowger's first-generation electromechanical design, which established a dedicated path through the switching matrix for the duration of the call, dominated the PBX market for the next eight decades. The 1970s saw the introduction of second-generation electronic PBXs that used computer technology to interweave up to 125 conversations on the same line by sampling each of them 8,000 times a second. Second-generation PBXs continued, however, to be "voice only": they lacked the speed and capacity to transmit data as effectively as leading-edge buyers were coming to prefer. Third-generation "voice-and-data" PBXs that avoided these problems did not become available until the early 1980s.

What is of primary interest about the PBX example is the fact that competitors that led in established technologies were slow to adopt new ones. AT&T, which had dominated electromechanical PBXs, trailed badly in the move to electronic PBXs. Rolm and Northern Telecom, which established substantial market presences on the basis of their second-generation voice-only PBXs, did not attempt to lead in the development of third-generation voice-and-data products: fringe players and entrants took on that role. And the successful voice-and-data pioneer, InteCom, displayed no interest in developing even newer PBXs with enough transmission capacity to handle video images as well as voice and data. To understand why technological leadership changed hands so often in the PBX industry, it is necessary to understand the nature of the substitution threat posed by later generations of technology to the sticky factors that had proved critical to competing effectively in earlier generations.

In the days of first-generation PBXs, the ability to achieve mechanical reliability had been critical. With electronic PBXs, high reliability could be achieved by using off-the-shelf components and building in redundancy. As a result, the ability to design software became critical. Successful software design remained an art, however: cumulated spending on it increased the likelihood of eventual success but did not guarantee it. To take just one example, IBM probably spent over $100 million in a failed attempt to develop a large, third-generation PBX; InteCom, in contrast, succeeded with less than $5 million in development expenditures.

With that background, it becomes easier to understand why PBX competitors made the choices that they did. The shift to electronic PBXs reduced the scarcity value of AT&T's ability, developed over several decades, to make extremely reliable electromechanical PBXs. While AT&T could still have moved aggressively into second-generation PBXs, its analysis indicated that this would increase customers' awareness of the new technology and hasten the cannibalization of its own large electromechanical rental base by enough to hurt its bottom line instead of helping it. Since the continuing opportunities for technological progress in PBXs and its discontinuous nature meant that AT&T could reenter the race later, it softpeddled electronic PBXs and concentrated on harvesting its electromechanical rental base.

Similarly, the successful second-generation competitors did not expect to have a big advantage at developing the next generation of PBXs. For that reason, and since they already had their hands full replacing the installed base of older electromechanical PBXs, they decided to leave third-generation demand to others, at least until that segment expanded significantly. Rolm, in particular, ploughed most of its profits into building up a network of marketing subsidiaries that were meant to allow it to defend its presence in PBXs in spite of continued technological progress by its competitors.

Finally, the successful voice-and-data pioneer, InteCom, did not attempt to make the next technological leap, to voice, data-and-video PBXs. That was because its founders sensed that that would be akin to betting what they had already achieved on their ability to hit consecutive home runs. Instead, InteCom's founders concentrated from the very beginning on skimming the market. While that strategy ultimately proved to be unsustainable, they laughed all the way to the bank, having recouped somewhere between ten and one hundred times their initial investment.

In summary, the PBX example reinforces the three principal messages of this section. First, the threat of substitution is a significant threat to the scarcity value of sticky factors. Second, this sort of threat is most likely to manifest itself against the backdrop of technological change. Third, while the threat of substitution can be combated by continuously upgrading or otherwise renewing the organization's stocks of sticky factors, such a policy is only likely to make sense when environmental change is cumulative in its effects. Changes that are expected to be discontinuous, in the sense of leveling initial differences in competitive position tend, in contrast, to make such a policy inadvisable.

Holdup threatens to divert scarcity value.

Even if the scarcity value of sticky factors can be preserved from imitation and substitution, the ability of the owners of the organization to appropriate the proceeds cannot be taken for granted. The possibility of expropriation is a consequence of the gap between ownership and control: there typically is such a gap, and it typically leaves room for self-serving behavior by nonowners. Such behavior can reduce either the owners' share of total scarcity value (holdup) or the total amount of scarcity value available to be divided among them and nonowners (slack), or both. The diversionary threat of holdup will be discussed in this section, and the dissipative threat of slack in the next one.

Holdup of the scarcity value of sticky factors by nonowners is a threat only to the extent that nonowners control the flow of services from other *cospecialized* (complementary and specialized) factors. To fix ideas, suppose that the owners control sticky factor A but not cospecialized factor B. Then, from the owners' perspective, the potential scope for holdup by those who *do* control the flow of services from factor B is simply the difference between the joint value of factors A and B and the sum of the values they can individually command (through redeployment) in the event of a failure to agree on terms for exploiting the complementarity. Note that factor B must be somewhat specialized as well as complementary to factor A to serve as the basis for holdup: if B were a totally general-purpose factor, the owners of the organization could costlessly redeploy away from it at the first hint of attempted holdup.

The extent of complementarity sets an upper limit on holdup; the lower limit is zero. The actual degree of holdup will vary between these broad limits in a way that depends on the influences listed below.

Contractual Arrangements. Owners can enter into contracts with nonowners who control cospecialized factors with a view to restricting the degree of holdup. Relatively comprehensive contracts that are cheap to enforce facilitate this purpose. However, totally comprehensive contracts enforceable at zero cost, the sorts of contracts that could theoretically eliminate holdup, are almost always impractical for reasons that include bounded rationality, uncertainty about the future and asymmetric information (Williamson 1975).

Dependence. Returning to the notation introduced above, there tends to be a significant difference between situations in which the value of factor A is more-or-less unilaterally dependent on the continued flow of services from factor B, and situations in which the dependence is bilateral. The degree of holdup tends to be higher in the former sorts of situations (when the owners of the firm are unilaterally dependent on nonowners) because such one-sidedness affords nonowners a more credible threat of defecting from the cooperative arrangement if their demands aren't met. While there are a host of measures owners can take to build up bilateral dependence, such as insisting that nonowners provide them with "hostages" (Williamson 1985), countermeasures are available to nonowners who would rather be able to hold up the owners than not.

Norms. The actual degree of holdup is more than just a matter of calculating what one can get away with: it depends on norms about what is fair, the extent to which promises should be kept and so on. Societal norms about acceptable levels of profit and the tendency to settle on focal points (e.g., the tendency in bargains between individuals to split the difference between initial offers) can also be lumped into this category of influences on the division of joint gains. The precise influence of norms is highly sensitive to the specifics of the situation.

Posturing. An interest group's perceptions of the value to it of reaching an agreement with the groups that control complementary specialized factors usually aren't completely known to all of them. This incompleteness of information creates room for posturing, or bluffing. Owners can posture as if a degree of holdup close to zero is the most they are willing to concede. Nonowners can engage in posturing as well, however.

An example will help make this description more concrete. It concerns the holdup of the owners of National Football League (NFL) franchises in the 1970s and 1980s.[8] The NFL consists of independently owned franchises that have managed, for the most part, to function as a cartel on the basis of selective antitrust exemptions. Since 1970, the NFL has weathered threats of imitation by the World Football League (WFL) and the United States Football League (USFL), each of which operated less than three seasons. It has withstood substitution threats to sustain much higher broadcast ratings than any other sport. As a result, it managed to sign lucrative multiyear contracts with the three TV networks in 1978 and in 1982, contracts that increased the total revenue available to the average NFL team by 77% in *real* terms between 1970 and 1984 (see Exhibit 5.5). In spite of this winning record, however, the average team's operating income fell by a third between those years. Why?

Holdup by NFL players seems to have been the principal reason for this decrease. People of the size, skill and recklessness necessary to play professional football are obviously specialized resources. The essential complementarity of their services to the scarcity value

Exhibit 5.5 The Distribution of Revenues for the Average NFL Team

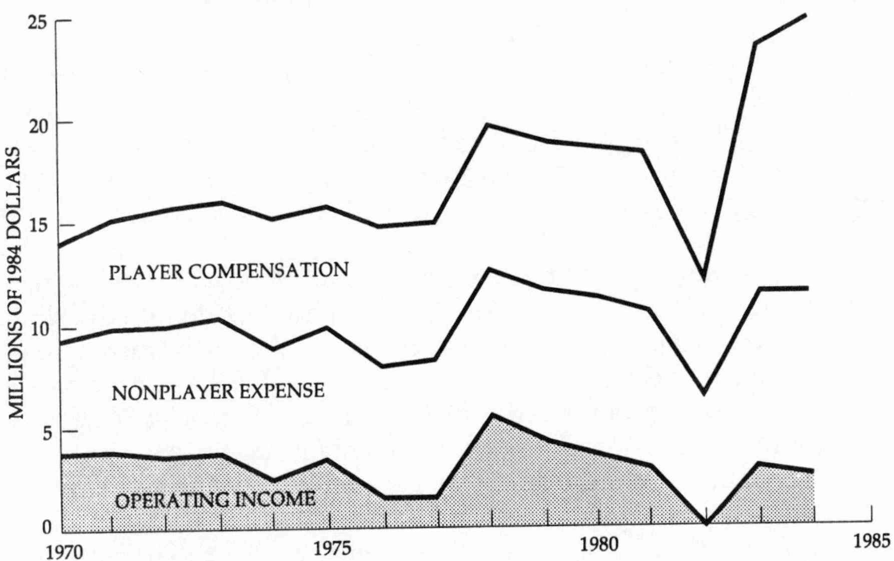

SOURCE: Porter (1986).

of football franchises has been evident from the inception of professional football: crowds of 70,000 people and more crowded into stadia as far back as the 1920s to watch stars such as Red Grange and Ernie Nevers.

Recognizing the resultant potential for holdup, the NFL evolved a number of practices to contain it. Players were signed to enforceable multiyear contracts that prespecified compensation levels. Arrangements were made to tilt the balance of mutual dependence in the owners' favor by keeping the players apart and the owners together: exclusive rights to draft rookies and restrictions on free agency by veterans increased the cost to individual players of not coming to terms; at the same time, revenue sharing among the owners blunted the incentives for them to engage in bidding wars for stars. The owners reacted to the formation of the NFL Players' Association (NFLPA) in 1956 by (a) studiously ignoring it; and (b) tripling salaries over the next decade in an effort that seems to have been designed, at least in part, to establish the norm that players would be treated fairly in individual bargaining. When demands for collective bargaining nevertheless proved irresistible, the owners cemented their own solidarity by requiring that any collective bargain be approved by at least three-quarters of them. The owners also adopted the posture of hanging tough when impasses occurred in the collective bargaining process, even at the risk of inducing strikes.

In spite of these measures, the NFL owners failed to prevent holdup by the players. Average player compensation climbed by more than 170% in real terms between 1970 and 1984. The players' share of total NFL revenues jumped from 35% to nearly 55%. The players captured, in effect, four-fifths of the increase in revenues per team over this period.

The reasons for this remarkable degree of holdup can be tied into the general influences on the degree of holdup identified earlier. The contracts signed by the players were obviously incomplete, given their limited duration. In fact, they *couldn't* have been made much more complete because of the constant churn of players in professional football and, more fundamentally, because it is impossible to contract for permanent ownership of (or more emotively, enslave) human capital. The various steps that the owners took to make their players more dependent on them were largely offset by the collectivization of bargaining (the NFLPA was certified as a union in 1971) and by the emergence, however short-lived, of alternative outlets for the players' services in the form of the WFL and the high-rolling USFL. The norms that the owners were trying to set for compensation levels failed to take hold with the players for a number of reasons: the average NFL career lasts less than five years; professional baseball and basketball players, who benefit from smaller rosters and less restrictive free-agency conditions, have tended to make almost twice as much per year as the average football player over a longer number of years; NFL franchises tend to have higher assessed values than other professional sports franchises. Finally, posturing by the owners did not work too well because, although they had more staying power than the players, they also stood to lose two to three times as much in absolute terms from strikes likely to follow posturing-related impasses. By the end of the 1980s, most NFL teams were reported to be losing money. They recently managed to secure another, even more lucrative TV contract, but it remains to be seen how much of the additional revenues will flow through to the bottom line.

In summary, the example of the NFL owners versus players reinforces the three principal messages of this section. First, holdup by those who control the flow of services from cospecialized factors is a significant threat to the ability of the owners of sticky factors to appropriate their scarcity value. Second, the degree of holdup is influenced by prevailing contractual arrangements, patterns of dependence, norms and posturing possibilities. Finally, while owners can pull on some or all of these levers to try to increase appropriability, at least some countermeasures are usually available to the would-be perpetrators of holdup.

SLACK THREATENS TO DISSIPATE SCARCITY VALUE.

Slack is the final threat to sustainability that must be taken into account. Slack measures the extent to which the scarcity value realized by the organization falls short of the amount potentially available to it. The conceptual distinction between slack and holdup is that the former shrinks the total size of the pie available to owners and nonowners while the latter shrinks the owners' slice of that pie. These dissipative and diversionary threats to the appropriability of scarcity value sometimes blend into each other in practice. For one thing, moves aimed at influencing the division of joint gains, such as posturing, can shrink the total amount of value available to be divided among owners and nonowners. For another, a certain amount of slack may be valued by nonowners, particularly employees, and therefore cannot be categorized as deadweight loss.

Slack cannot, by definition, be less than zero. An upper bound on it is implicit in the condition that organizations cannot sustain losses indefinitely. As a result, particularly valuable product market positions can be expected to afford the most scope for slack. Or in plainer language, rich diets tend to lead to a hardening of organizational arteries. Estimates of the fraction of revenues dissipated, on average, in this fashion tend to range from 10% to 40%.[9] These estimates hint at both the significance of slack and the difficulty of measuring it precisely.

Slack stems, in fact, from measurement problems, broadly defined. More precisely, slack is attributable to the difficulty of monitoring the uses to which nonowners put the complementary factors under their control. Such difficulties are apt to be particularly severe for factors that Alchian and Woodward (1988, p. 69) have termed *plastic:* factors in regard to which "there is a wide range of discretionary, legitimate decisions within which the user may choose." Plasticity is a prominent feature of creative industries of the sort discussed in the section on substitution threats. It should also be pointed out that factors that are vulnerable to holdup can be quite implastic, containing the threat of slack. Alumina refining provides an example. An alumina refinery is typically cospecialized to particular inputs and therefore vulnerable to holdup by, say, the local government imposing a bauxite levy or hiking power prices. It is far less vulnerable to slack, however, because its operating technology implies that it must be run close to flat out. (The only real alternative, shutting it down, isn't usually likely to further the interests of the nonowners who get to influence that call.)

The example of the alumina refinery is, of course, rather special in that plasticity, and the slack it leads to, is usually less predetermined and more something to be managed. It is easy to see why there is room for creativity in this regard. Slack is the by-product of a misalignment of owners' and nonowners' interests. If only a more perfect union could be effected between them, that would make things better all around by increasing the total size of the pie. The rash of recent writings on how to do so can be boiled down to three recommendations: gather more information, use that information to offer nonowners incentives, of both the stick and the carrot variety, that are more compatible with owners' interests and employ moral suasion as well since nonowners tend to be motivated by more than just the prospects of pain or gain. All of this is fine as far as it goes. What usually goes unsaid in the how-to literature, however, is that such devices cannot wipe out slack because of information-gathering costs, limits to the ability of organizations to offer high-powered (market-like) incentives and the incomplete efficacy of moral suasion.[10] Slack has to be managed and minimized, but it has its own logic, and is therefore impossible to eliminate. The analysis must take it into account, particularly when strategic options differ significantly in the degree of slack they are likely to induce.

Once again, the analysis of a case will help illustrate this particular threat to sustainability. The case concerns Xerox in the copier business over roughly the last two decades. The information assembled (from public sources) in Exhibit 5.6 indicates that the 1980s have marked a period of substantial turnaround for the company. Its managers seem to have achieved these improvements largely on the basis of the devices described earlier. They compared Xerox to its Japanese competitors and to "best-practice" companies in other industries. They used the information gleaned from such benchmarking to establish targets for improvement and incentives to

Exhibit 5.6 Xerox's Copier Business in the 1980s

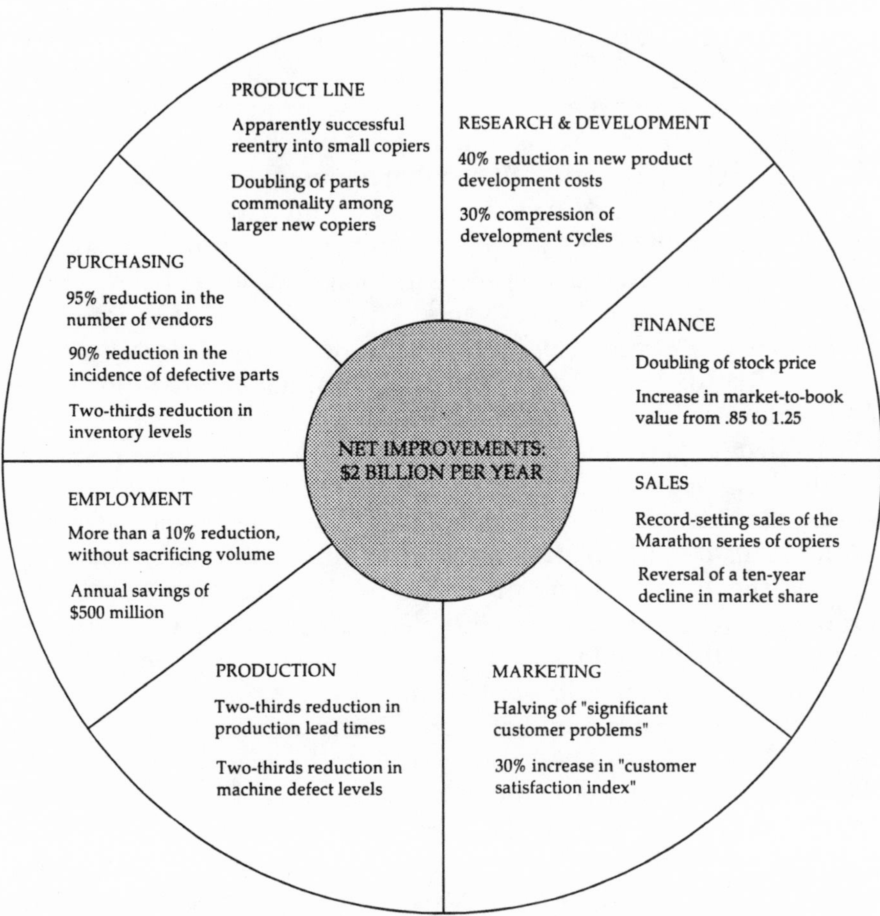

achieve them. And they reinforced these incentives by trying to create an organizational culture that emphasized quality, responsiveness and other good things. While Xerox still has a long way to go, its top managers deserve to be congratulated for the progress they have made in repositioning the company since 1980.

It is also clear, however, that Xerox could not have wrung such significant improvements out of its copier business in the 1980s unless it had accumulated stupendous amounts of slack there in the 1970s. Xerox's own statements about the savings achieved in the 1980s as well as other estimates (e.g., Bresnahan 1986, p. 59) suggest that by the late 1970s, slack was dissipating at least 20%

of the company's sales revenues. If this figure were applied just to the second half of the 1970s (and slack implicitly assumed to be zero in the first half), it would suggest total slack of about $5 billion over those five years, an amount greater than the operating income Xerox recorded over that period. While these are *very* soft numbers, their suggestion that Xerox squandered much of its birthright in the 1970s is strongly borne out by what happened to its shareholders during the 1970s and early 1980s. According to a study by Ball (1987), Xerox ranked last among the 50 largest mature U.S. companies in terms of the fraction of its income that actually translated into incremental shareholder value. Thus, the ratio of shareholder enrichment to retained earnings over the 1970s and early 1980s was −220% for Xerox, compared to an average of +84% for Ball's entire sample!

This dismal performance can readily be linked to the framework for thinking about slack that was presented earlier. I shall simply sketch the analysis. There was a lot of potential for slack at Xerox in the 1970s because it started out with a monopoly on a booming market (the Xerox 914 had proved to be the single most profitable product in U.S. history), a stranglehold on plain-paper copying technology that would sustain its uniqueness for at least a few more years, and a few additional years of implementation lags before any imitators/substitutors that found a way around Xerox's thicket of patents could make themselves felt in the market place. There were several reasons why much of this potential for slack became reality. The plasticity of the factors Xerox deployed in the copier business, as indicated by its innovation-intensity and the 5-to-1 ratio of support staff to assembly-line workers, made it hard to monitor. Monitoring was further complicated by incomplete information about such things as segment sizes, shares and relative cost positions, and by higgledy-piggledy growth (the number of Xerox employees increased from 3,000 in 1963 to 60,000 in 1970, and came close to doubling again in the next decade). That the growth was faster than had been anticipated and that numerous lawsuits were launched threatening Xerox with dismemberment exacerbated the challenge confronting its managers.

Some readers may still be inclined to ascribe the stupendous amount of slack at Xerox in the 1970s to the ineptitude of its top management instead of the informational complexity of the situation that they faced. In particular, Peter McCulough, whose tenure as Xerox's CEO coincides with some of the darkest days for the company's copier business, has been pilloried for introducing a matrixed organizational structure that ultimately proved to be so unwieldy that it had to be abandoned. This seems more than just a tad unfair. The powers that were at Xerox, including McCulough's predecessor, Joseph Wilson, were convinced by the second half of the 1960s that the company's operations were outstripping its ability to control them, and that much more elaborate controls were needed to prevent them from flaming out like a gigantic Roman candle.[11] Tom Peters, who worked on one of McKinsey's many consulting studies for Xerox toward the end of McCulough's tenure, has this to say about the company's move to increase control-through-monitoring (*BusinessWeek*, June 22, 1987, p. 106):

> It was a classic case of doing everything right. They hired people from three of the best-managed companies, IBM, Ford, and General Electric. . . . But there is nothing harder to deal with than success.

In summary, while the example of Xerox in the 1980s suggests that slack can be managed at the margin, its experience in the 1970s reminds us that it is very hard to curb the strong predispositions toward slack implied by substantial potential scarcity value and high monitoring costs. By implication, irreducible slack is something that a careful analysis of sustainability must take into account, especially when strategic options differ significantly in terms of the plasticity of the factor bundles associated with them.

SUSTAINABILITY ANALYSIS SHOULD BE INTEGRATED WITH POSITIONING ANALYSIS.

The examples used to illustrate the four threats to sustainability—the cigarette and PBX industries, the NFL and Xerox—were meant to dramatize the shortsightedness of ignoring issues of sustainability in the pursuit of superior market positions. That drama should not, however, be misinterpreted as an indication that they grossly overstate the extent of unsustainability. All four examples illustrate scarcity value leaking away, to a significant degree, over a 10- to 20-year period. This pattern is consistent with the evidence presented at the beginning of this chapter on the rapid convergence of profit rates toward average levels.

The implication, clearly, is that it is important to think through sustainability ahead of time instead of taking it for granted. Sustainability is not, however, the Holy Grail: claiming such an exalted status for it would contradict chapter 1's lesson that there are no generic success factors. More analytically, a focus on sustainability at the expense of the positioning considerations that were discussed in the last chapter would unduly devalue "hit-and-run" strategies of the sort successfully practiced by InteCom. And a focus on sustainability at the expense of the considerations of flexibility that are discussed in the next chapter would unduly favor committing sooner rather than later.

By implication, sustainability analysis should be integrated with the other sorts of analysis discussed in this book. The analysis that led Du Pont to preempt expansion opportunities in the U.S. market for titanium dioxide in the 1970s will help illustrate the sort of integration that is required.[12] Titanium dioxide is a commodity chemical used as a whitener in paints, plastics and paper. It can be manufactured with batch-process sulfate technology that uses low-grade ilmenite ore or continuous-process chloride technology configured to handle either ilmenite or higher-grade rutile ore. In 1970, the two chloride processes were at cost parity with each other but enjoyed an advantage over the older sulfate process.

Environmental shifts in 1970 and 1971 drastically altered the cost positions of the three titanium dioxide production processes (see Exhibit 5.7). In Australia, restrictions were imposed on the mining of rutile from beach sands, forcing up its price by more than 70%. And in the United States, more stringent emissions standards increased waste disposal costs, particularly for the sulfate process, which was the dirtiest of the three.

Du Pont was the only competitor that had learned how to operate the chloride process with low-grade ilmenite ore. It now found itself blessed with a very sizeable cost advantage. Additionally, this advantage looked very sustainable. Mastery of the ilmenite chloride process was a black art: it could be achieved only by investing $50 million to $100 million and several years in testing an efficiently scaled plant. Du Pont expected that the cost and risk of this alternative would keep its competitors from imitating its demonstrably superior technology. Substitution did not seem to be much of a threat either. Although a way of enriching ilmenite into a feedstock suitable for the rutile chloride process might be developed, it would not be able to match the economics of Du Pont's ilmenite chloride process. While there might be some holdup by

Exhibit 5.7 Standard Costs of 50,000-Ton Titanium Dioxide Plants*

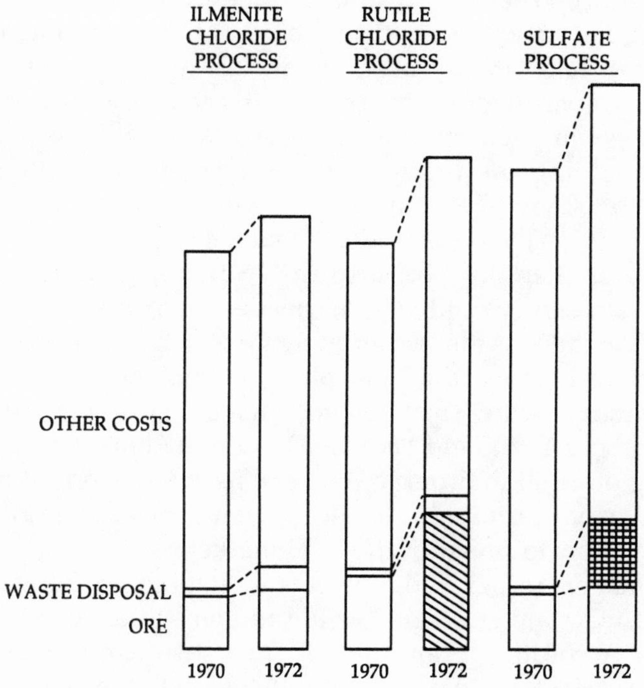

*Plants are assumed to operate at capacity, which is possible only after several years of "shake down."

SOURCE: Ghemawat (1984)

suppliers of labor and ilmenite ore, neither of these factors was cospecialized enough to Du Pont's proprietary know-how to appropriate much of its scarcity value. Finally, once this know-how was embodied in capacity, it became relatively implastic, limiting the threat of slack.

Based on positioning and sustainability analysis, Du Pont decided, in 1972, to invest more than $200 million to add 200,000 tons of capacity at a new site to preempt all the growth in U.S. demand forecast through 1985. This capacity was to be added in the form of two 100,000-ton lines. Du Pont expected that completion of the second line would raise its market share to a commanding 65%.

By 1975, however, faltering demand forced Du Pont to defer the construction of the second of the two planned lines indefinitely.

Because of corporate capital constraints and differential inflation rates that had reduced the cost advantage of new ilmenite chloride capacity, reservations also began to surface about the first line, on which $10 million had already been spent. Key managers at Du Pont's Pigments Department spent five months simulating the discounted cash flows implied by two alternate strategies: "growth," which involved adding the first line at the new site for a target 1985 market share of 55%, and "maintain," which did not.

Naive positioning analysis favored the maintain strategy for discount rates greater than 13% because the extra capacity implied by the growth strategy would not be needed immediately. The relevant cost of capital was almost certainly greater than this break-even discount rate because the data plugged into the cash flow analysis were nominal rather than deflated (at a time when inflation was running at about 10%), and because Du Pont had just imposed capital rationing on itself in order to preserve its AAA bond rating. By implication, naive positioning analysis would have suggested abandoning the effort to preempt the U.S. market.

Du Pont's managers recognized, however, that its choice between the growth and maintain strategies would influence the actions of its competitors. According to an internal Du Pont memorandum, if it did not increase its share of the expanding market, "Competitive expansion and the resulting scramble for sales will affect price. . . . Du Pont would then no longer be an industry leader and would be facing the prospect of competing on a 'me-too' basis." The growth strategy was likely to enhance sustainability by denying competitors the opportunity to add efficiently scaled new capacity and learn how to operate it. Du Pont reckoned that by keeping competitors' costs high, the growth strategy would permit long-run prices 3% higher than could be expected of the maintain strategy. When this differential was factored into the analysis, the break-even discount rate for picking the growth strategy over the maintain strategy increased from 13% to 20%. Du Pont decided to go ahead and preempt. Fifteen years later, it is still the only operator of the ilmenite chloride technology. It is also in the midst of a ten-year program to double its capacity at home and abroad that has already made it the largest producer of titanium dioxide worldwide.

This account has focused, so far, on Du Pont's calculation of the value of doing one thing as opposed to another. What lay behind the numbers? Du Pont apparently understood that the (potentially) scarce sticky factor it had going for it was its knowledge about how to operate the chloride process with low-grade ore and took actions to preserve that (intangible) factor's scarcity value. These included not only the preemptive addition of capacity but also the complementary actions of acquiring additional supplies of low-grade ore, not licensing proprietary technology, keeping prices low in the short run and otherwise signaling the aggressiveness of its expansion plans. By implication, advance consideration of sustainability can facilitate not only the selection of the right course of action but also its implementation.

Du Pont obviously deserves considerable credit for the analysis that it performed. The one thing it can be faulted for, however, is its initial failure to take uncertainty seriously. For instance, aggregate demand for titanium dioxide could be expected to have a significant influence on the profitability of the capacity Du Pont planned to add, given the price-inelasticity of the former and the capital-intensity of the latter. Yet Du Pont worked with single-point forecasts of demand through 1975. It was taken by surprise when demand that year fell 25% short of the forecast level, and nearly ended up canceling its plans to expand at a new site. It was not until 1976 that it began to pay explicit attention to the possibility that its forecasts might not pan out.

The tendency to suppress uncertainty and focus on a single possible outcome is widespread. The next chapter discusses why and how this trap should be avoided.

Summary

The sustainability of superior product market positions rests on factor market imperfections of the sort implied by commitment to sticky factors. Such sticky factors must continue to be scarce over time and the owners of the organization must be able to appropriate some of their scarcity value. Scarcity value is threatened by imitation and substitution, and appropriability by holdup and slack. Analysis of these threats should be used to modify the baseline economics derived from positioning analysis.

6

→>> <<←

Flexibility: The Value of Recourse

> Information is merely the negative measure of uncertainty. . . . When there is uncertainty, there is usually the possibility of reducing it by the acquisition of information.
>
> —Kenneth J. Arrow, *The Economics of Information*

Positioning and sustainability analyses share a simplifying assumption, namely, that the organization will persist forever with the strategic option it initially elects to pursue. In other words, both positioning and sustainability analysis assume zero revisions. Flexibility analysis relaxes this assumption: it takes into account the revision possibilities offered by each option. An example will illustrate why this generalization is essential.

Reconsider the replacement of Old Coke with New Coke.

The best way to illustrate the importance of flexibility analysis is with a cautionary tale of a company failing to think through revision possibilities ahead of time. The tale concerns Coca-Cola's reformulation, for what turned out to be just a few months in 1985, of its flagship brand. Coca-Cola's dominant brand of soft drink, Coke, was important to it for much the same reasons that the dominant brand of cigarettes, Marlboro (discussed in the last chapter), was important to *its* proprietor, Philip Morris. In industries built around intangible mass-market images, such as soft drinks and cigarettes, profitability hinges on ownership of one of the largest brands around. The Coke brand had lost several points of U.S. market share, a matter of no small importance given that each point lost wiped out more than $200 million in sales of above-average profitability. Coca-Cola's new management team focused on Pepsi-Cola's flagship brand, Pepsi, as the culprit.

The biggest weapon in Pepsi's competitive arsenal, everyone agreed, was its much-advertised ability to beat Coke consistently in blind taste tests. In the late 1970s, however, researchers on the Diet Coke project had stumbled across a new sugar-based cola formula that looked as if it might fare better against Pepsi. Roberto Goizueta had supervised that research team; when he became chief executive officer (CEO) of the Coca-Cola Company in 1981, he authorized tests aimed at ascertaining whether the old formula, synonymous with the company for nearly a century, should be replaced with the new one.

Replacement seemed to make sense in terms of positioning. The old formula was losing out 2-to-3 to Pepsi in blind taste tests, primarily because it was appreciably less sweet. The new formula was somewhat sweeter than the old one. It beat the old formula by 55% to 45% in blind testing, and Pepsi's formula by a somewhat narrower margin. The positioning-related arguments for this shift toward the "center" of the sweetness spectrum appeared to be reinforced by the way the Diet Coke brand was coming to dominate the low-calorie flank of the market.

These positioning considerations tended, however, to be contradicted by considerations of sustainability. The theory of competition in brand space makes it clear that particular brand "locations" can sustain above-average returns only to the extent that it is difficult to relocate brands.[1] In image-intensive consumer product categories, the difficulties of brand relocation consist, for the most part, of the difficulty of satisfactorily repositioning an image in the consumer's mind. As a result, proprietors of already-successful brands in such industries tend to avoid tinkering with their images for fear of undermining sustainability: while there may be some shift, over time, in the content of successful brands, there is rarely explicit reference to it in the imagery surrounding them. Thus, while the sugar and caffeine content of the Coke brand had been altered in the past, Coca-Cola hadn't tried to draw the public eye to the previous reformulations. Hyping up the replacement of Coke's old formula with the new one would shatter these precedents by entailing a very visible shift of image.

There is no reason to think that Coca-Cola's managers ignored such concerns. They were evidently convinced, however, that the company's best course of action, on balance, was to replace the formula and to do so with a lot of fanfare. One reason was that the new formula did especially well with subjects who knew that they were tasting a new Coke flavor. The new formula then beat the old one by 61% to 39%, more than twice the differential recorded in blind taste tests. Another reason was that a substantial amount of free publicity could be drummed up by pitching the reformulation as a major event. There were other supposed benefits as well, such as the perception that a bold move would help reestablish Coca-Cola bottlers' respect for the company's marketing expertise. According to the published accounts, Coca-Cola's best guess was that a highly publicized reformulation would, over a three-year period, increase the share of its flagship brand by about three percentage points. The benefits of this expected increase in sales appeared to outweigh expected repositioning costs of over $100 million *and* sustainability-related concerns. Coca-Cola chose to go ahead and make a very quick, visible switch to the new formula so as to have it available in most of the country in time for the 99th anniversary of its old one, May 8, 1985.

With the benefit of hindsight, that was clearly the wrong call. The stock market was skeptical from the very start. On the day that Coca-Cola called a press conference to announce the reformulation (April 23, 1985), its market value fell by $213 million, while Pepsi-Cola's rose by $176 million. The rise in Pepsi-Cola's stock anticipated, in part, the speed with which it was able to exploit Coke's switch to promote itself. Within a week of Coca-Cola's press conference, it had aired an advertisement on national TV depicting a forlorn Coke fan about to drink her first Pepsi because Coke was no longer "the real thing." Consumers were the next group to balk. Although curiosity on their part pushed up sales of reformulated Coke in May, Coke shipments fell by as much as 15% in key southern markets in June, and by July, consumers' reported preferences were running 2-to-1 in favor of the old formula over the new one. As a result, Coca-Cola bottlers, who had been generally supportive of the reformulation even though they knew they would have to shoulder much of its direct costs, began to turn against the new formula as well.

The writing was on the wall. On July 11, 1985, Coca-Cola undid four-and-a-half years of planning by publicly apologizing for scrapping its 99-year-old formula and announcing that the old formula would be revived as "Coca-Cola Classic" and sold alongside the new one. By August, this move had been rationalized as an integral part of the megabrand (multiproduct) strategy for Coke. But this rationalization did little to change business realities, particularly the fact that new Coke was proving to be a bust. Despite earlier assurances by its managers that the reformulation would pay back its costs *in 1985* by increasing sales, Coke lost 1.5 points of domestic share that year, and the company's overall operating margin on soft drinks fell to 16.0% from 17.5% in 1984. More importantly, the long-term prognosis for new Coke was distinctly unhealthy. Exhibit 6.1 traces its subsequent slide: by 1989, new Coke had fallen off the list of the ten best-selling soft drinks. It had also, according to the *Wall Street Journal*, won the unwelcome title of "the Edsel of the 1980s."

Obviously, a lot of what would happen in the event of reformulation was uncertain at the time Coca-Cola made its move. While

Exhibit 6.1 Soft Drink Market Shares

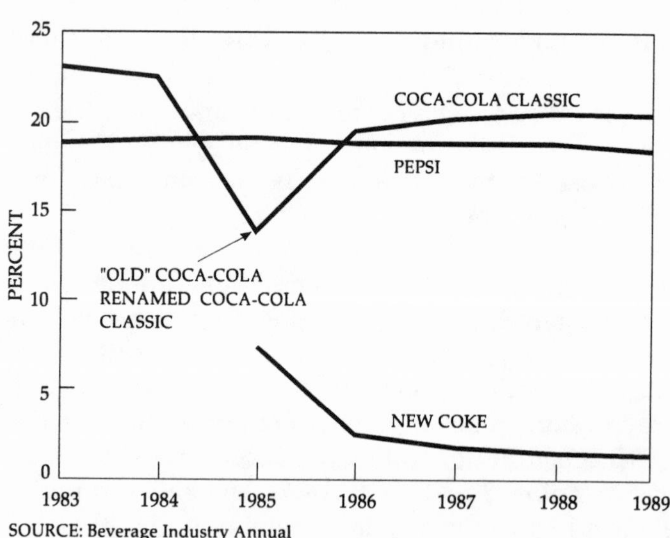

SOURCE: Beverage Industry Annual

flexibility analysis wouldn't have eliminated these uncertainties, it *would* have given Coca-Cola a firmer grip on them. Let me introduce some notation so that I can be more precise. Define A as the strategic option of repositioning Coke in the customer's mind as a sweeter cola (the option that Coca-Cola initially elected to pursue) and B as the strategic option of not doing so. The analysis up to this point can be summarized by noting that option A was favored by positioning considerations such as the results of the taste tests, and option B by considerations of sustainability. In spring 1985, Coca-Cola chose option A; a few months later, it revised its course of action by switching to option B. Flexibility analysis is meant to help managers think through the possibilities of such revisions ahead of time.

Coca-Cola's choice did not account for revision possibilities because the company failed to take uncertainty seriously. Its CEO described the highly publicized reformulation, at the time it was undertaken, as "our surest move ever." More broadly, the people in charge at Coca-Cola seemed to have convinced themselves that the most extensive test marketing in company history had unambiguously established the superiority of option A to option B, eliminating the need to account for uncertainties that might reverse the initial rankings of the two options and perhaps even lead the company to revise its initial choice between them. There are two respects in which things might have gone better with some flexibility analysis.

First, flexibility analysis would have forced Coca-Cola to think through the contingencies that confronted it ahead of time. Even if there were no way, given the complexity of the unfolding situation, to avoid the A-to-B flip-flop, thinking through contingencies would have helped Coca-Cola handle the flip-flop more adroitly than it actually did. In announcing the initial choice of option A, for instance, Coca-Cola might have harped less on how the old formula had been sealed up in a bank vault *never to be used again*. In flopping back to option B, Coca-Cola might have done better if it hadn't been unprepared to deal with the contingency *most likely* to prevail if it did have to revise its initial choice, namely, what to do with new Coke. Only recently did it announce plans to test market new Coke as Coke II, positioned head-to-head against Pepsi-Cola's flagship brand. Some think this will work; others think it won't. The point is that Coca-Cola probably wouldn't have taken five years to decide what to do with new Coke if it had thought through contingencies ahead of time.

Second, flexibility analysis might have persuaded Coca-Cola not to make the initial choice that it did. Coca-Cola's annual report for 1985 defended the very visible and very embarrassing reformulation, its initial choice of option A, as evidence of its flexibility in responding to demand shifts in the United States. Actually, what flexibility analysis, as discussed in this chapter, would have clarified was that option B appeared to afford substantially more flexibility value in spring 1985 than did option A.

The reasons bear some explanation. The prospects for Coke's old formula were actually highly uncertain in early 1985. First of all, it wasn't clear whether the share slippage in the early 1980s was caused by Pepsi's comparative taste testing or simply reflected partial cannibalization of the flagship brand as a side-effect of Coca-Cola's new megabrand strategy. In fact, the Coke megabrand had reached an all-time high by picking up over four points of domestic share since the introduction of Diet Coke in 1982, more than twice as much as the Pepsi megabrand. Second, even if it could be established that the old formula *was* being challenged successfully by Pepsi, it wasn't clear that replacing it with fanfare would improve matters. The test-market sample of nearly 200,000 people across the country was compromised by its generally equal weighting of the daily Coke six-packer and the occasional and fickle drinker of soft drinks. Even worse, the test marketing slurred over taste-independent components of brand image: in the interests of secrecy, even when the new formula was identified as a new Coke taste, subjects were never told that it might entirely supplant the familiar old one. Finally, the general view, dramatized by horror stories such as the dire fate of the Schlitz brand of beer since the mid-1970s, is that many reformulations do not succeed as planned. Taken together, these considerations suggest that there was substantial ambiguity about whether Coke's old formula had a taste problem and, if so, whether a very visible reformulation (option A) would improve matters.

This ambiguity wasn't, of course, fixed. The megabrand strategy was still new enough in 1985 that updates on its progress or lack thereof could be expected to prove very informative. Coca-Cola could also have secured extra information through additional experimentation, such as introducing the new formula without any fanfare into perhaps just a few markets. In contrast, option A, which Coca-Cola actually pursued, represented a very costly way of acquiring information to resolve the ambiguity about whether to reposition

Coke's consumer image. As noted above, the flip to option A involved out-of-pocket repositioning costs of over $100 million: these would be unsalvageable if it didn't work out. The costs required to flop back to option B in the event that option A failed would probably be even greater, perhaps by a factor of two or three. Additionally, the loss of face from a very visible flip-flop, while incalculable, could hardly be expected to be inconsequential. Option B, in contrast, afforded much more flexibility value in the sense that it would be easier to revise. If the positioning-cum-sustainability values of the two options had come out close (without Coca-Cola's cooperation, we have no way of knowing whether the company thought they did or not), differences in the revision possibilities associated with the two options would have broken the near tie in favor of option B. Given what the initial choice of option A led to, that would not have been a bad thing.

Revisions tend to be common.

The Coca-Cola example is far from exceptional. Revisions of initial choices, even commitment-intensive ones, tend to be quite common: very few choices lock the organization at once and for all time into a particular course of action. When the degree of commitment implied by a strategic choice is less than total, it cannot be treated as a strictly terminal act. Attention must also be paid to the revision possibilities associated with each strategic option. Yet few organizations seem to account for revision possibilities in making the choices that they do.

Evidence that revisions tend to be quite common can be adduced by citing additional cases. For example, in the case discussed toward the end of the last chapter, Du Pont initially planned to add two 100,000-ton lines for producing titanium dioxide at a new location. Three years later, in the face of faltering demand, it revised that initial choice by indefinitely deferring the construction of the second of the two lines. It thought about abandoning the first line as well, but ultimately decided not to do so.

The conclusions from individual cases can be reinforced with cross-industry evidence on the revision rates associated with specific types of commitments. A sample of capacity expansion announcements for several chemicals indicates that 25% of the announced expansions were never carried out, another 12% were delayed by more than one year, and 13% involved significantly less capacity than originally announced. Over 70% of new consumer brands never make it past the test-marketing stage. And revision rates for research and development programs seem, if anything, to be even higher.[2]

Confronted with such data, most managers accept the necessity of thinking through revision possibilities ahead of time. Very few of the organizations they are attached to actually do so, however. This assertion obviously applies to organizations that fail to make any allowance at all for uncertainty: in the absence of uncertainty, there would be no need to change one's mind about what to do. And most of the methods that *are* used to account for uncertainty take the course of action to be predetermined and focus on the cash flows expected from it.[3] Flexibility analysis, in contrast, focuses on expectations of changes in expectations and how, if at all, the organization should revise its course of action in light of such changes.

I should add that flexibility analysis does not supplant the analysis of expected values. Expected cash flows, derived from positioning and sustainability analyses under the assumption of zero revisions, remain an essential input to any sensible comparison of strategic options. As explained in the next section, however, they do need to be supplemented with assessments of the revision possibilities afforded by each option. Disregarding revision possibilities would devalue courses of action that expand the organization's future strategic choices—a matter for serious concern since such expansion potential seems to account for a significant fraction of the market value of many businesses.[4]

Revision possibilities afford flexibility value.

The *flexibility value* of a strategic option is defined as the extra value expected from being able to take advantage of the revision possibilities it offers as opposed to persisting with it through thick and thin. This section will begin by illustrating flexibility value in the context of a stylized example, continue on to a business application, and conclude by formalizing the concept.

Coin Tosses

Consider a coin-tossing game in which you receive a dollar if you call a toss correctly and must pay one if you don't. You can play this game with one of two coins. You know that one coin is equally likely to come up heads or tails. The other coin is weighted, but you aren't sure about either the degree or direction of its bias. With which one would you prefer to play?

If you get to call just one toss, you should be indifferent between the two coins: both offer you an even chance of winning as opposed to losing one dollar. The choice between them becomes interesting, however, with two (or more) tosses. If you can observe the outcome of the first toss before calling the second one, you should *always* opt for the biased coin. The biased coin makes more sense because, unlike the fair coin, it affords flexibility value. With the biased coin, gains can be achieved by conditioning the second-round call on the first-round outcome instead of prespecifying both calls. The value of flexibility turns out to equal the degree of bias, suitably normalized. With zero bias, flexibility is worth nothing. With maximum bias, of the sort implied by a coin that has either two heads or two tails, flexibility adds a dollar of expected value: you can always get the second call right after observing the first one, implying a 50% chance of making two dollars and a 50% chance of breaking even.

This example should serve as a reminder that a strategic option has flexibility value not because it is a sure thing but to the extent that it is an abundant store of potentially valuable revision possibilities. Most people would describe the fair coin as safer, since the probability of it coming up heads as opposed to tails is known right from the beginning. It offers no flexibility value, however, because the outcome of the first toss yields no information relevant to the call on the second toss. With a coin known to be biased, in contrast, the dominant strategy is to observe the outcome of the first toss and bet, irrespective of initial plans, that it will be repeated on the second one. By implication, flexibility in the sense being discussed here isn't synonymous with safety or security.

Venture Capitalism

Flexibility was worth one dollar in the case of the maximally biased coin. The venture capital industry illustrates that it can be worth millions of dollars in real settings. The typical venture capital firm receives thousands of investment proposals each year.[5] It pursues a few hundred of these leads in some depth, and ultimately commits its capital to ten or fewer of them. For all the care that goes into selecting them, however, the funded few generate disappointing returns more often than not: the industry rule of thumb seems to be that only 10% to 15% of the ventures in the typical capitalist's portfolio turn out to be clear winners.

Venture capitalists have dealt with these long odds by developing a number of practices that afford them flexibility value. Perhaps most important, they infuse capital into the new venture in several stages instead of committing it all up-front. Each new stage is generally linked to some significant development in the history of the venture: completion of design, pilot production and break even are examples. While the amounts disbursed are dictated by business requirements, they tend to increase substantially from one stage to the next *if* the venture capitalist continues to supply capital.

Staged capital commitment is valuable to venture capitalists for exactly the same reason that the ability to observe the outcome of the first toss of the biased coin before calling the second one was valuable in the coin-tossing example. Staged commitment lets the venture capitalist decide whether to put more into or pull out of the venture after learning more about whether it is a plum or a lemon. Stevenson, Muzyka and Timmons (1987) have simulated the difference this can make in the context of two-stage venture capital investments. Exhibit 6.2 summarizes their findings, for typical

Exhibit 6.2 Simulated Returns for Venture Capital Funds

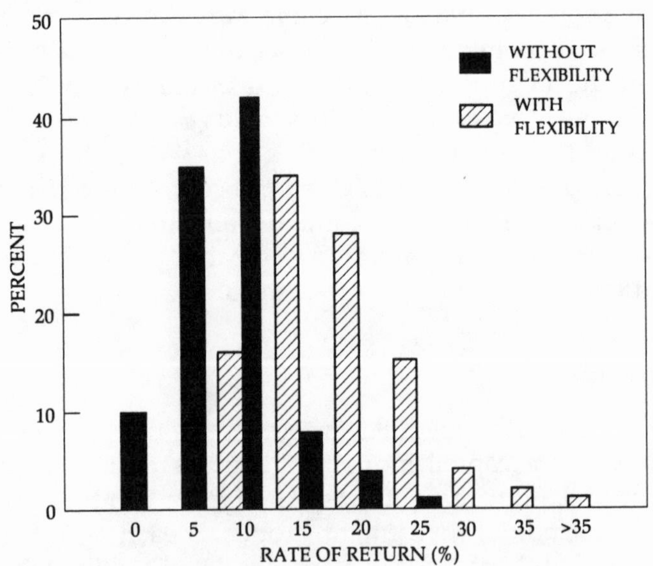

Source: Howard Stevenson, Daniel Muzyka, and Jeffrey Timmons (1987).

parametric values, about the utility of being able to condition the second-stage investment on the basis of information obtained during the first stage. Note the plausible inference that venture capitalism would not be viable without flexibility.

Staged capital commitment is valuable to venture capitalists because it preserves the possibility of abandoning the venture. While good news about the venture obviously improves the expected value that the capitalist assigns to it, it is the possibility of receiving *bad* news about it that makes flexibility valuable. That is because if the information received about the venture weren't bad, there would be no reason to revise support for the venture and therefore no value to commitment in stages as opposed to all at once.

Formalization

Flexibility value has been discussed so far in the context of specific examples. It is time to formalize the concept. Consider, because it parallels the structure of the two examples, the two-stage choice that is depicted in Exhibit 6.3.[6] There are two strategic options, A and B. The first choice between them is made at time 0. Feedback is received at time *t* about whether the initial choice is still appropriate or not; if it isn't, it is revised. How should the revision possibilities

Exhibit 6.3 Revision Possibilities

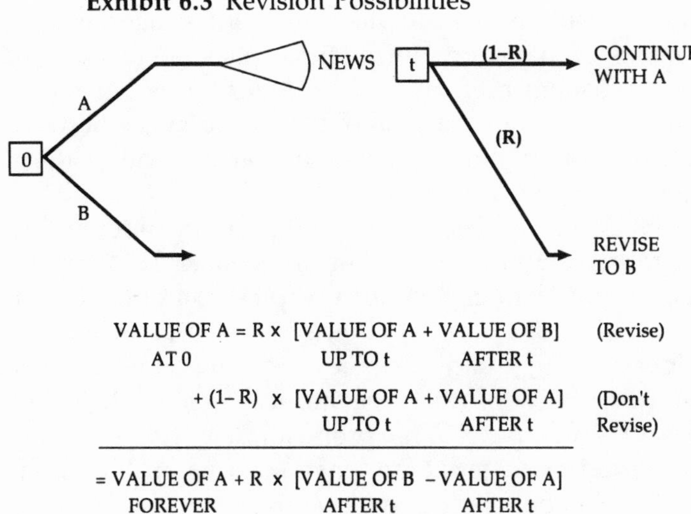

afforded by the two options down the road be factored into the *initial* assessment (at time 0) of their values?

I shall evaluate just one of the two options since the other can be analyzed in exactly the same way. What is the value to the organization of picking option A at time 0? It can stick with A forever (or at least until it goes bankrupt) if it likes: this is the value of option A without revision possibilities. It may be able to do better with recourse, however, if it receives news unfavorable enough to A to make it want to revise its choice to B in spite of the costs of changing its mind. This possibility underlies flexibility value. The *total* value of picking option A at time 0 is calculated in Exhibit 6.3. In words, it is equal to the value of A forever *plus* the probability of revision multiplied by the expected value of revision if that possibility becomes a reality. The first term, the value of option A forever, assumes no revisions and is therefore a measure of expected value to be derived under the assumptions of positioning and sustainability analyses. The second term, in contrast, is of value only if revision does occur and can therefore be thought of as a measure of flexibility value. The equation in Exhibit 6.3 indicates that these two measures can be added to get to the total value expected of each strategic option.

Two implications of this equation deserve to be spelled out. First, its structure transcends the assumption of any specific attitude toward risk. This is useful because of the disagreement about whether managers generally love or fear risk. Compare, for instance, the attitudes of two eminent economists on this subject. While John Maynard Keynes considered nearly all investment a manifestation of the animal spirits of managers, John Hicks, his student, devised the dictum that managers prefer the quiet life. One is left with a strong sense that this tells us more about the differences between these eminent economists rather than about any broad patterns across managers.

Second, the equation implies that flexibility is an independent source of value rather than just a stopper in the sink. This positive value depends, as noted in the venture capital example, on the possibility of regretting one's initial choice so much as to want to revise it. The idea isn't that bad news is good news. Instead, it is that, given the inevitability of mistakes and a degree of flexibility, bad news is better than no news. This proposition is entirely consistent with the reported managerial tendency to focus on the downsides of alternatives in considering uncertainty.[7]

Flexibility analysis should be integrated with positioning and sustainability analyses.

The valuation equation also implies that flexibility value can be added to (expected) positioning-cum-sustainability value to get to an estimate of the total value of a strategic option. The simplicity of the representation may make this exercise sound easier than it actually is. It deserves to be discussed in more detail, and illustrated. This section undertakes the first task and the next section the second one.

Recognizing Uncertainty

The analysis must recognize and explicitly represent uncertainty. This point may seem too obvious to be worth registering, especially since nearly all large U.S. companies claim, in surveys, to allow for uncertainty in making the choices that they do.[8] The same surveys also suggest, however, that the claimed allowance mostly involves fudging single-point forecasts. The Du Pont and Coca-Cola cases are both illustrations. And even when multiple possible outcomes are considered, they usually aren't integrated into the process of choice. This problem seems particularly severe in relation to strategic choices.

The tendency to suppress uncertainty is no accident. It reflects, in part, individuals' overconfidence in their own predictions about the future.[9] It also has an element of persuasion that Savage (1971, p. 799) has evoked particularly well:

> The usual tests and language habits of our culture tend to . . . encourage not only the vice of acting and speaking as though we are certain when we are only fairly sure, but also that of acting and speaking as though the opinions we have are worthless when they are not very strong.

In spite of the psychological pangs that it seems to induce, there is no alternative to the recognition and explicit representation of uncertainty. Nothing can be gained by fooling oneself about the probabilities, except a false sense of security.

Constructing Scenarios

Coin-tossing examples notwithstanding, the typical strategic choice has an infinite number of possible outcomes. It is useful to crystallize these possibilities into *scenarios,* a limited number of possible futures selected so as to be interestingly different. The coarse grain of scenarios permits in-depth consideration of revision possibilities in a way that would be much harder, if not impossible, to achieve with a finer-grained characterization of future possibilities (as is often attempted in computer simulations). In addition, aficionados often claim that the concreteness of scenarios broadens the consideration of uncertainties by stretching as well as focusing the mind.[10]

The scenarios selected from the continuum of possibilities should satisfy two main criteria. First, they should be possible but extreme. More specifically, they should be different enough that one option doesn't outshine the rest across all scenarios. Second, each scenario should be internally consistent. Schoemaker (1991) has recently proposed a number of tests that are helpful in this regard: consistency with trends, in terms of how correlated uncertainties are resolved, and with the inclinations of those in a position to influence the eventual outcome. In a particularly interesting application, Porter (1985, chap. 13) uses similar tests to construct scenarios for the future structure of the chain saw industry.

Although it is never easy to invent the future, the *logic* of scenario construction is fairly straightforward. Identify the key uncertainties that will determine the relative attractiveness of the strategic options being considered. Compound these uncertainties in ways different enough to favor different options, and test the resultant scenarios for internal consistency. Iterate until you have a few (generally two to four) scenarios that bound the uncertainties and satisfy consistency constraints. In the special case where people start out by focusing on *success scenarios* congenial to the courses of action that they favor, this implies confronting them with *failure scenarios* based on unfavorable rather than favorable resolutions of key uncertainties. The inclusion of a devil's advocate in the group performing the analysis has been reported to be helpful in this regard.[11]

Analyzing Positioning and Sustainability

Once scenarios have been constructed, the next step is to analyze the implications of each one for the positioning-cum-sustainability value of each option. It is also useful, at this juncture, to account for the ways in which the organization's choice among its options might affect the likelihood of different scenarios coming to pass. The objective is to assess the first term on the right-hand side of the equation presented in the last section, namely the value of a strategic option persisted with forever.

The first term in the equation is an *unconditional* expectation in the sense that it is supposed to be averaged across favorable and unfavorable outcomes. The step discussed here involves forming expectations that are *conditional* in the sense of being predicated on specific scenarios, and that must therefore be weighted by probabilities and summed to yield the unconditional expectation. This two-step estimation procedure is useful because most people seem to find it easier to form conditional expectations than unconditional ones.[12]

Since it is often possible to adjust strategic options as well as revise them, and since flexibility analysis deals only with revision possibilities, this is also the proper place to think about how each option might be adjusted to unfavorable scenarios without being revised. The *adjustability* of a strategic option helps insure its positioning-cum-sustainability value. Such insurance tends, however, to be costly and to provide only limited protection. This last point can be illustrated with the sad story of the billion-dollar tractor factory that Deere started up in Waterloo (Iowa) in 1981. The very high capital costs reflected extensive automation aimed, in part, at easing adjustment to shifts in the mix of demand for tractors. The pitfalls of the robotized, tightly integrated design became evident, however, when aggregate demand for tractors slumped. The new factory couldn't be shut down in parts, so Deere had to operate it at utilization rates as low as 10% and yet incur the labor and energy costs necessary to keep the whole operation going. The "factory of the future" that was supposed to be adjustable to small changes had turned out to be very unadjustable to larger changes.[13]

Analyzing Flexibility

The last step in the analysis involves looking at revision possibilities. The infinite number of points in time at which a strategic option might be revised forces a focus on points at which important news is expected or jumps in the level of commitment planned. Revision possibilities are particularly valuable in the vicinity of such points because of the improvement of information in the first instance and the impending loss of flexibility in the second. Venture capitalists recognize this when they define the stages at which they commit (or cut off) capital to a venture in terms of significant developments in its history.

The revision possibilities afforded by a specific option at a specific point in time can be evaluated by assessing the extra information about the option that is likely to become available by that point and the usefulness of incorporating the extra information into the choice between persistence and revision. When several possible revision points have to be considered, as is likely in the case of multistage investment options, the evaluation should proceed backward in time. Consider, as a concrete example, a three-stage venture capital investment. Theory suggests starting out by solving for what the capitalist should do in stage 3, conditional on the information likely to be available to him if he gets there. The stage 3 outcomes that are expected as a result should be folded into the analysis of the stage 2 problem, and so on. Caution must be exercised, however, in stringing together long chains of this sort. As *The Economist* (September 30, 1989, p. 76) put it, "Proceeding with loss-making Mega-Widgets Mark-1 on the strength of unlimited profits from 1995's Mark-4 looks like the sort of risk few companies can afford to take—no matter how well their executives did at business school."

Instead of trying to estimate the flexibility value afforded by an option directly, it is sometimes useful to think of it as the negative measure of the commitment implicit in the initial choice of that option. The general characterization of commitment contained in chapter 2 comes in handy here: it reminds us that flexibility value can be reduced not just by lock-in, but also by lock-out, implementation lags and inertia. Note that this upsets the simple idea, based solely on considerations of lock-in, that investment always reduces flexibility while not investing always preserves it. The next section contains an example in which continued investment is the more rather than less flexible option.

The integration procedure can be illustrated.

The example I will use to illustrate how considerations of positioning, sustainability and flexibility are to be integrated is based on a consulting assignment. My client held excess capacity for producing a chemical that I will refer to as crypton, and was looking for new market outlets. Laboratory research suggested that crypton might be used to advantage in the formulation of certain industrial solvents. A group was commissioned to study this opportunity in more detail.

The study group concluded that crypton-based solvents might avoid some of the environmental problems and associated costs-in-use of conventional solvents *and* be slightly less expensive to produce. It also thought that a competitive advantage based on crypton would be sustainable to a significant degree. The company was the sole manufacturer of crypton and would retain its monopoly position for at least six more years, until its patents on the composition of that chemical expired. Afterwards, competitive encroachment was expected to be limited by various advantages that the company would have secured by moving early.

A full-time business team was set up, as a result, to put together a plan to exploit the opportunity in solvents. The team painstakingly assessed the potential for competitive advantage from crypton in each segment and deliberated on how that potential might best be exploited. After considering the margin-volume combinations that seemed to be attainable, it came to the conclusion that the business would create more value by giving up much of the extra margin theoretically available to crypton (in segments where it had an advantage) than by "value pricing" and limiting volume. It also concluded that the emphasis should be on selling crypton-based solvents rather than crypton, for two reasons. First, independent solvent-sellers were unlikely to make the investment required to prove the new technology, diffuse information about its performance and overcome the costs to their buyers of switching. Second, lack of forward integration would preclude price discrimination between segments in which crypton was worth a lot and those in which it was worth little.

The business plan submitted by the team translated these conclusions about volume, costs and prices into the first explicit analysis of the economics of the proposed business. The "base case" forecast was that its return on investment (ROI) would exceed 70% in year 5. The plan also reported the results of several tests of the sensitivity of this forecast to higher costs and lower prices than assumed in the base case. These tests individually reduced the forecast ROI by three to fifteen percentage points. They had more of a depressing effect if taken together, but only to a level that still looked healthy. Funding for the proposed business was approved.

During year 1, it became clear that success wouldn't be as swift as forecast in the original plan. Technical problems looked as if they would limit sales volume that year to a fraction of the level originally forecast. The business team was confident, however, that these problems were temporary. The next plan that it prepared, toward the middle of the year, forecast that sales volume would be back on track by year 3. The revised set of estimates did not, as a result, raise questions about the economic attractiveness of continuing funding.

By year 2, it had become clear that the technical problems were far more serious than originally anticipated. Virtually no solvents had been sold in year 1, and year 2 sales looked as if they would amount to less than one-tenth of the level originally forecast for year 1. As a result, the business team reduced its volume forecasts by three-quarters for year 3 and by one-half in the long run. It predicted that the business would be able to achieve a positive net present value in spite of the reduced volume. The committee in charge of new businesses wasn't so sure and commissioned a thorough review. I was enlisted to help.

As I learned more about the analysis the business team had conducted, what struck me the most was its focus on a single outcome involving technical success and commercial acceptance. The new business was attempting to develop a new product for a new market. The overwhelming majority of such attempts fail. Yet the analysis had effectively ignored this possibility. Having convinced itself that the new business was a good idea, the business team had tried to make the "strongest" possible case for it by not dwelling on the possibility of failure. This had come to hurt its credibility. The committee in charge of new businesses had lost confidence in the numbers the team was running past it, figured that any future surprises were very likely to be negative ones and had therefore begun to think of cutting its losses. The only way of rebuilding the committee's confidence seemed to be to give adverse uncertainties their due.

The team was inclined to think that it had already accounted for adverse uncertainties in the sensitivity tests it had performed. The trouble with these tests was that they had simply tweaked the basic success scenario in far too limited a way to alter the rankings of the two options, funding and abandoning the business. To force explicit consideration of the possibility that continued funding might not be the best course of action, we hammered out a failure scenario based on pessimistic rather than optimistic assumptions about the resolution of technical and commercial uncertainties. The failure scenario that we settled on reduced the long-run volume forecast to one-quarter of the level assumed in the (revised) success scenario.[14] Recalculation of the net present value of continuing along the investment path described in the business plan under these lower volume assumptions yielded a large negative number. By implication, if we had been certain at the time that the failure scenario was the one that would come to pass, it would have made sense to abandon the new business right away.

Having estimated the conditional expectations for the strategic options under the assumption of zero revisions, it was time to get a feel for revision possibilities. The abandonment option, once selected, was unlikely to be revised any time soon because the business team would be dismembered and doubts raised internally and externally about the company's capabilities in and commitment to the solvent market. In contrast, the option of continuing funding *did* offer significant revision (abandonment) possibilities, which it proved convenient to organize in terms of the three stages depicted in Exhibit 6.4. Stage 1 would involve experimentation in the broad sense of formulating crypton-based solvents, gaining trial by a few

Exhibit 6.4 The Entry Strategy

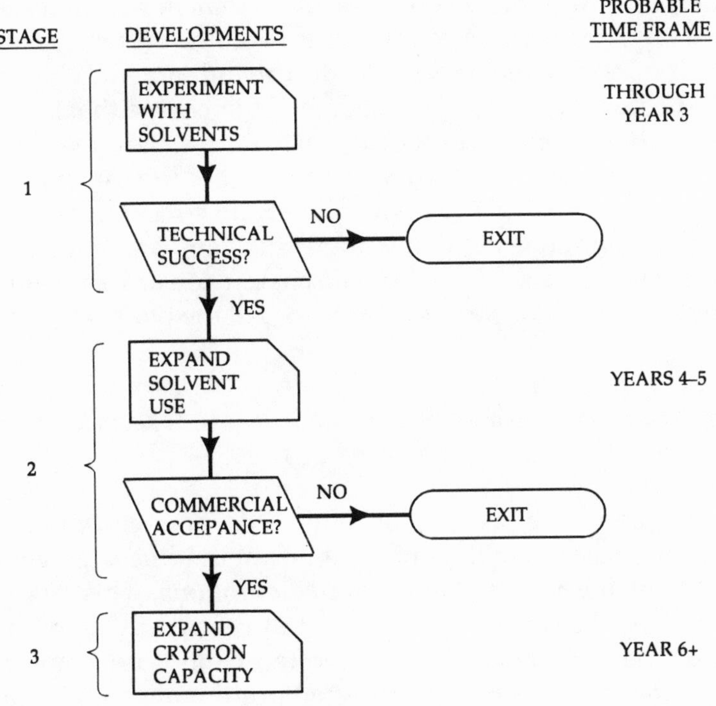

lead buyers and working out the technical problems that were bound to crop up. Technical success would lead to stage 2, which involved expanding in solvents. Broad commercial acceptance of crypton-based solvents would exhaust the excess crypton production capacity with which the company was starting out and trigger stage 3, which involved the addition of a new crypton production line.

An expensive new line for producing crypton would make sense only if the chemical made a big splash in solvents, i.e., if both stages 1 and 2 succeeded. The possibility of revising stage 3 plans was therefore valuable to a degree dependent on the improvement of information over stages 1 and 2 about the long-run prospects for the business. With perfect information expected by the end of stage 2 about which of the two scenarios was materializing, the probability of technical and commercial success had to be only about 15% to justify continued funding, compared to a level, probably unrealistic, of 40% in the "no additional information" case. And even with less-than-perfect information expected at the end of stage 2, the value of securing additional information seemed large enough to justify continued funding, at least through stage 1.

This review of the business concluded with an attempt to ensure that flexibility was availed of instead of remaining an abstraction. The business team was asked to set up volume and margin hurdles which, if missed, were likely to lead to abandonment. This arrangement reflected the sense of the committee in charge that by scheduling new businesses to run out of cash unless they met targets, it could enhance both the information content of the forecasts submitted to it by the business team and the team's incentives to achieve them. The committee felt that without such an arrangement, investment renewal biases of the sort discussed toward the end of the next section would make it very hard to pull the plug on the venture.

Flexibility is particularly valuable in the presence of ambiguity and learning possibilities.

The example in the last section illustrated how considerations of positioning, sustainability and flexibility should be aggregated into estimates of the total value of strategic options. This aggregation is always feasible in principle. It isn't always easily accomplished, however, because flexibility value often cannot be pinned down in a way that can be added to expected positioning-cum-sustainability value. How, in such cases, should one proceed?

Note, first of all, that there is no problem if positioning-cum-sustainability analysis and flexibility analysis both favor the same strategic option. It is in cases where they conflict that it becomes necessary to trade one off against the other. This section sheds light on that trade-off by identifying the conditions under which the flexibility afforded by revision possibilities is apt to be especially valuable. Situational analysis of whether these conditions are satisfied will sharpen one's sense of how the comparisons based on positioning and sustainability analyses have to come out for a particular strategic option to be adopted or rejected.

The two conditions that make flexibility especially valuable are informational ones evident in the coin-tossing example discussed earlier. Why was the possibility of revising the call on the second toss worthless in the case of the fair coin but worthwhile in the case of the biased coin? One reason for the difference was related to the probability distribution of possible outcomes, which was known for the fair coin but assumed to be *ambiguous* for the biased coin. If the probability that the biased coin would come up heads as opposed to tails were known right from the beginning, revision possibilities wouldn't be worth anything in calling tosses of it either. The second reason was related to *learning*. Something could be learned about the outcomes of future tosses by observing the outcome of the first toss in the case of the biased coin but not in the case of the fair one.

The coin-tossing example also suggests that ambiguity and learning are linked. Ambiguity bounds learning and learning reduces, over time, the amount of ambiguity. The two do have somewhat different correlates, however, and therefore need to be elaborated on separately.

Ambiguity

The notion of ambiguity should be made precise. Exhibit 6.5a illustrates a situation in which there is uncertainty but no ambiguity about what will happen: the underlying probability distribution of outcomes (to an action) is known. Exhibit 6.5b illustrates a situation in which there *is* ambiguity. Note that ambiguity encompasses variability in beliefs about the probability distribution of outcomes as well as variability in the outcomes themselves. Ambiguity leaves open the possibility of learning more about the true probability distribution.

There is an element of ambiguity to most strategic choices because

Exhibit 6.5a Uncertainty Without Ambiguity

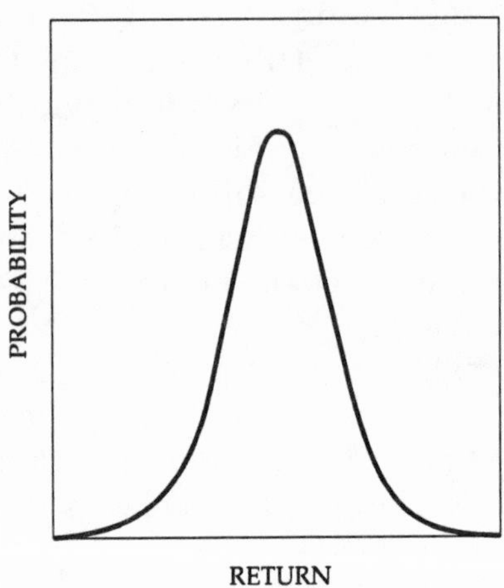

Exhibit 6.5b Ambiguity

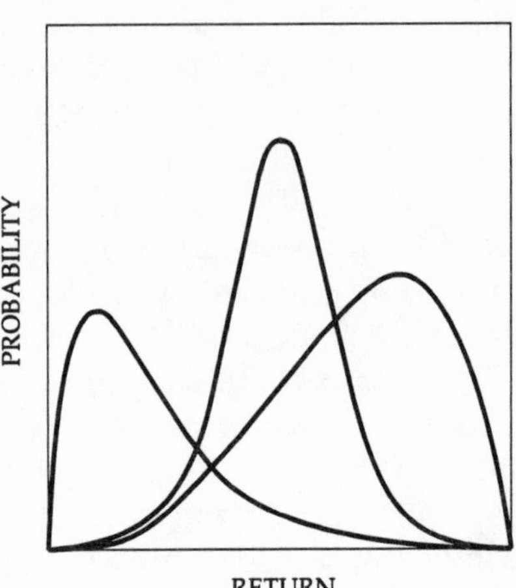

it is usually hard to calibrate the relevant probabilities on the basis of either common sense or repeated observation. What is of interest in deciding whether to expect a lot out of flexibility analysis, however, is specification of the situations in which ambiguity is likely to be particularly high. Most such specifications have revolved around one (or occasionally, as in Duncan (1972), both) of two factors, *complexity* and *radicality*.

Complexity is high if pulling one thread causes many others to move as well.[15] This sort of overlap of causal structures is likely to exacerbate the constraints of bounded rationality and enlarge the extent of ambiguity. Radicality may reflect either a first-of-a-kind option or an environment undergoing (uncertain) structural change. The radicality of a situation implies that the prior information on it is apt to be poor.

The role of both factors is illustrated by the RAND Corporation's postmortem on the capital costs of 44 chemical plants that pioneered process technology (Merrow, Phillips and Myers 1981). Since these were innovative investments that, on average, contained five separate process steps, cost $175 million (in 1980 dollars), and took seven years to complete, they obviously involved both complexity and radicality. As one might expect, their capital costs were pretty ambiguous *ex ante*.

One way to see this is to compare the record of the pioneering efforts in the RAND sample with more conventional chemical projects. Chemical engineers conventionally divide projects for chemical plants into four phases, each spanning one or two stages of cost estimation: R&D (stage 0), project definition (stage 1), engineering (stages 2 and 3) and actual construction (stage 4). Engineers also have conventional rules of thumb for the "confidence interval" at each stage: stage 0 cost estimates, for example, are thought of as varying by as much as 40% from actual capital costs; stage 4 estimates, in contrast, are expected to be within 5% of the true value. Their usual zone of confidence is traced out as the shaded triangle in Exhibit 6.6.

If these rules off the conventional rack had fit pioneering plants of above-average complexity and radicality, the data points for the latter would all have landed in the triangle, with averages close to the broken line that bisects it. That wasn't what happened: only a minority of the data points, and *none* of the stage averages, fell within the zone of conventional confidence.[16] In other words, extra ambiguity was evident in the choice of whether to build a pioneering chemical plant as opposed to a conventional one.

A second, more precise way of pinpointing the role played by

Exhibit 6.6 Accuracy of Estimates for Pioneering Plants

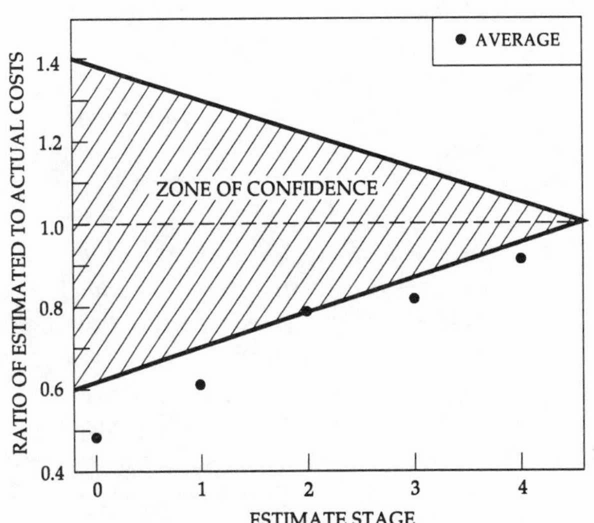

SOURCE: Merrow, Phillips, and Myers (1981).

complexity and radicality is to make comparisons in this regard *within* the sample of pioneering plants. After using multiple regression techniques to pay bolts out of the blue—accelerating inflation, revised regulations, and other acts of God—their due, the RAND researchers found that much of the variation in estimate quality within their sample could be pinned on two factors. The first factor that led the engineers astray was the degree of coordination required in building each plant, measured as the number of continuously linked process steps it contained. Such coordination requirements signaled complexity in this instance because they mandated interactive as well as individual analyses of the process steps. The second factor that degraded the engineering estimates was the plant's degree of novelty, measured by the extent to which it used commercially unproven technology. Such novelty obviously proxies radicality. So there is some solid evidence to support the notion that complexity and radicality tend to make for above-average ambiguity.

Learning

Ambiguity is necessary but not sufficient for there to be learning. It is the possibility of changing one's mind intrinsic to the latter that makes flexibility valuable. Learning depends on timely feedback, which may be obtained freely (e.g., through the exogenous unfolding of events) or at the cost of experimentation. Some degree of access to feedback of a high signal-to-noise ratio is essential to learning, and sooner is better than later.

The two factors that make for learning, feedback and timeliness, can usefully be collapsed into a *learn-to-burn* rate. The rate at which useful feedback is received about whether the chosen course of action is the right one (the "learn" rate) goes into the numerator, and the rate at which commitment to the chosen course of action is piling up (the "burn" rate) goes into the denominator. Since the examples in this chapter were selected so as to illustrate the importance of flexibility, the options in each one were analyzed primarily in terms of their learn-to-burn rates. In the crypton example, for instance, the new business was continued rather than discontinued because it offered a high learn rate (like most new ventures) and required only a low burn rate because of the existence of excess capacity for producing crypton at an efficient scale.

Learning does not, of course, occur automatically, not even for new ventures. The extent to which it takes place depends on how the option that is pursued is actually managed. Time, Inc.'s short-lived launch of *TV-Cable Week* is an instructive example.[17] Over a period of five years, Time twice considered and twice rejected the idea of launching a weekly cable TV listings guide that would be comarketed with cable operators. The idea ran up against the heterogeneity of market segments. It wouldn't be easy to produce a system-specific guide for hundreds if not thousands of cable systems that operated in different time zones, offered different menus, and spread them across different channels. But in fall 1981, two freshly minted MBAs were told to reexamine the idea. Recognizing the complexity of what was involved, they pegged start-up costs at $100 million (the largest such amount in publishing history) and figured that a 60% market penetration would be needed to justify the investment. This figure represented five times the highest penetration ever achieved by a mass-market magazine. Accordingly, they recommended that if Time did go ahead with *TV-Cable Week,* it should start with a six-month, $9-million market test.

Incredibly enough, Time's top management decided, in January 1982, to go ahead *without* a market test. The go-for-broke aspects of this approach were compounded by the upfront commitment of setting it up in a new, nonunionized location and by hyperbole about the company's "deep pockets commitment" to the venture. Launch proceeded as planned, in spring 1983. By the time *TV-Cable Week* was folded, in September 1983, it had signed up fewer than 20 cable systems (out of the 4,000+ in the United States) at a cost to the company of about $50 million. In the weeks that followed, Time's stock lost $750 million in market value. Taking a more flexible approach by conducting a market test wouldn't have made *TV-Cable Week* work, but it *would* have increased the learn-to-burn rate, saving Time money and face.

One thing Time does deserve credit for, though, is its prespecification of a secret "bail-out" scenario. This scenario presumed failure, described three points at which *TV-Cable Week* might be abandoned and estimated the losses abandonment would entail: $10 million by January 1983, $38 million by June and $59 million by the end of the year. In spite of the worsening news about the venture, the first two checkpoints came and went without triggering abandonment. Time did pull the plug, though, before it passed the third checkpoint—even though the "base case" scenario had framed *TV-Cable Week* as a five-year investment program that would demand $100 million of corporate cash before it returned any. This is fairly effective handling of a difficult administrative situation if one believes that organizations tend to get trapped into losing courses of action, often spending more on them in failure than the amount initially budgeted for them under success scenarios.[18] Specific consideration, in advance, of the revision possibilities afforded by the option of launching *TV-Cable Week* without a market test probably helped Time limit its losses.

The *TV-Cable Week* example reinforces a point made earlier in this chapter, in the context of the crypton study: advance consideration of flexibility aids not only the analysis of strategic options but also the implementation of the option that *is* selected because it improves the likelihood that the revision possibilities afforded by that option will be taken advantage of. The *TV-Cable Week* examples suggests, in addition, that flexibility analysis can significantly aid implementation even when the option that is selected is inflexible compared to the alternatives. Finally it, together with several of the other examples presented in this book, serves as a reminder that there is always room for error in how the analysis ranks strategic options. Coping with such error is the topic of the next chapter.

Summary

Uncertainty is endemic to strategic choices. Positioning and sustainability analysis can be used to estimate the expected value of a strategic option under the assumption of zero revisions. That assumption needs to be relaxed, however, because revision possibilities represent an independent source of value. The flexibility value inherent in them can, in principle, be added to expected positioning-cum-sustainability value to get to an estimate of the total value of a strategic option. Flexibility is particularly valuable when there is considerable ambiguity and the possibility of cost-effective learning.

7

-»» ««-

Judgment: Coping with Error

The question about the sources of our knowledge . . . has always been asked in the spirit of: 'What are the best sources of our knowledge—the most reliable ones, those which will not lead us into error, and those to which we can and must turn, in the case of doubt, as the court of last appeal?' I propose to assume, instead, that no such ideal sources exist—no more than ideal rulers—and that *all* 'sources' are liable to lead us into error at times.

—Karl Popper, *Conjectures and Refutations*

The last three chapters discussed a procedure for estimating the total value of strategic options. It is also necessary, however, to consider the possibility of error in the evaluations. Some of that error can be eliminated by testing the rankings that emerge from positioning, sustainability and flexibility analysis for consistency with prior beliefs, or by incorporating these priors into the analysis. Error has an irreducible component as well, though, that challenges the organization to strike a balance between making too many bad commitments and passing up too many good ones. This chapter elaborates on the possibility of error and its implications.

Errors in the analysis may be either honest mistakes or deliberate distortions.

There is always the possibility of error in the implementation of *any* analytical procedure. The analysis of positioning, sustainability and flexibility is no exception. The errors that creep into it can be dichotomized by intent, into mistakes and distortions.

Mistakes are hard to generalize about because of their accidental, varied character. I *will* mention two sorts of mistakes, though, because of their specific links to the analytical framework developed in the last three chapters. First, strategic analyses typically emphasize considerations of positioning at the expense of those of sustainability and flexibility. This is probably attributable to the extent to which the assumptions that underlie positioning analysis, zero differential reactions and zero revisions, simplify matters. Whatever the reasons, this tendency will, unless checked, undervalue strategic options that promise to cement a superior competitive position or open up future possibilities. Second, such analyses often focus on success scenarios—on how things are going to work out—without explicitly recognizing as much. That is one of the reasons why a certain amount of sophisticated skepticism on the part of the reviewers is in order.

Deliberate distortions can be discussed more systematically because of the motives that underlie them. Distortions are possible because of information asymmetries within organizations. Such information asymmetries are most simply examined in terms of a simple paradigm within which an agent analyzes the strategic options and his or her principal chooses among them. This paradigm suggests three sorts of distortions that the principal must keep in mind.

The first sort of distortion stems from *imperfect monitoring* by the principal of the agent(s)'s level of effort at generating information. Imperfect monitoring typically leads to some shirking on the part of those who are supposed to exert themselves. In the context of strategic choice, there are many ways for the agent to restrict his or her efforts to generate information. Most involve limiting the (presumably costly) search for alternatives to the strategy that is in place: by waiting to observe a discrepancy instead of actively rooting out options for strategic change, by restricting the number of options considered, or by concentrating on options about which it is easy to generate information (such as those that require only minor modifications to the current strategy). This tendency will, unless checked, lead the organization to change its strategy too slowly.

The second sort of distortion stems from *imperfect observation* by the principal of the information that the agent has generated. The agent will typically be expected to edit the information available to him or her before transmitting it to the principal. Imperfect observability implies that the agent will be able to bias organizational choice by simply not transmitting enough information to make serious candidates of the strategies he or she does not personally desire to see implemented. And in anticipation of such editing, the effort-averse agent will not allot much effort to generating information about undesired strategies. Examples of strategies that might tend to be suppressed as a result include contractionary strategies, strategies that reduce the intraorganizational power of the agent's subunit and strategies that call the agent's earlier recommendations or choices into question. Unless checked, this tendency will, from the organizational perspective, overemphasize pain aversion.

The final sort of distortion stems from *imperfect verifiability* of the information that does get transmitted to the principal. An agent with some preferences over the strategic options he or she serves up for higher-level consideration will have an interest in structuring the analysis so as to "sell" his or her preferred one. Imperfect verifiability implies the ability of the agent to get away with some salesmanship, for reasons that include direct auditing costs, the ambiguity that enshrouds strategic choices and the logrolling that accompanies them. Salesmanship can show up in the analysis in a relatively innocent guise (for instance, in the formation of necessarily subjective judgments); it can also involve outright falsification on the part of the agent. It is ubiquitous enough to have inspired Brealey and Myers' (1984, p. 244) Second Law: "The proportion of proposed projects having a positive estimated NPV [net present value] is independent of top management's estimate of the opportunity cost of capital." Unless salesmanship is curbed, it will degrade the usefulness of the analysis to the extent that the agent's preferences diverge from the organization's.

For all these reasons, it is impossible to be certain that the option favored by the evaluation procedure is actually the one worth pursuing. One way of figuring out how to cope with this problem is to consider a setting in which the connection between forecast and actual values is *particularly* tenuous.

CONSIDER BIDDING PATTERNS ON OFFSHORE OIL AND GAS LEASES.

Consider the record on the offshore oil and gas leases that the U.S. government has auctioned off since 1954. According to the rules of the game, oil companies or consortia submit sealed bids on a tract-by-tract basis. Tracts are awarded to the highest bidders, who then stump up the amounts bid, shoulder further exploration and development costs, and pay royalties at a prespecified rate on any revenues from production.

The oil companies have long understood the logic of basing bids for tracts on estimates of their value and have come up with a number of ingenious techniques for evaluating prospective properties. Seismic mapping is the most important one. It involves setting off explosions that send shock waves through the earth's crust, measuring the speed with which the waves are reflected, and using that information (and high-speed computers) to make rough maps of the underground rock strata. Such maps are combined with contingent rules for estimating production potential and costs, and with forecasts of future oil prices, into estimates of the total value of each tract. Each participant's value analysis of each federal sale typically runs to several filing cases.

Filing cases of data notwithstanding, tract valuation leaves a lot of room for judgment. The Alaska North Slope sale, in 1969, is the classic example. Atlantic Richfield and Humble were partners in most of the pre-bid seismic exploration and therefore shared essentially the same information about tract values. They evaluated and acted on it independently, however. Exhibit 7.1 plots their bids on the 55 tracts that both bid on. Note that the correlation between the two is almost zero: they fell within a factor of two of each other's bids in less than one-third of the tracts. At one extreme, Humble bid 17 times more than Atlantic Richfield, and at the other, only one-thirtieth as much! By implication, bidders on offshore tracts can be counted on to hold widely divergent opinions even about what should be common values.

This divergence of opinion poses a serious problem. It means that oil companies cannot afford to base their bids on a tract solely on their private estimates of its value, not even if they can count on those estimates being unbiased (on average). If they took only their private estimates of value into account, they would be subject to a statistical phenomenon known as the *winner's curse.* Note that there will be a tendency for the bidder with the largest estimate

Exhibit 7.1 Alaska North Slope Sale

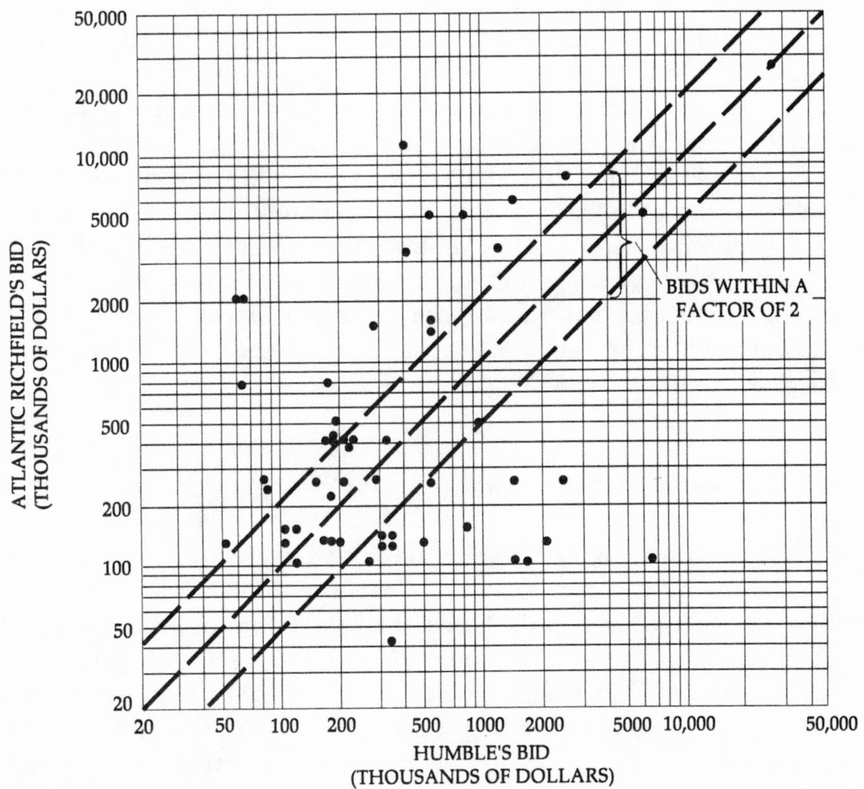

to make the highest bid. As a result, even if estimates are unbiased, the winner will find, on average, that *its* estimate was too high.

In order to combat the winner's curse, oil companies combine their analysis of tract values with other information in deciding how much to bid. For one thing, they do not average out the level of competition across all tracts. Instead, they sort tracts into three or four categories based on the number of bids each is likely to attract, and shade their bids the most on the tracts where they expect the most competition because it is in such settings that the winner's curse is likely to wreak the most havoc.[1] They also consider asymmetries in information between themselves and other likely bidders. Such considerations are particularly important in the case of "drainage" tracts, which are adjacent to tracts that have already been drilled.[2] Bidders who aren't neighbors (i.e., haven't drilled on adjacent tracts) exercise caution in bidding on drainage tracts because wresting them away from better-informed rivals compounds the probability of having overestimated tract values. That leaves a lot of money on the table for neighbors to pick up, which they do.

These adjustment procedures are somewhat specialized to bids on offshore oil and gas tracts. What is of broader interest is the idea of supplementing the analysis of value with information that has only an indirect bearing on it. Whether one expects to encounter zero competitors on a particular tract or a dozen doesn't directly affect the value of the reserves buried beneath it. Neither does better or worse information than one's competitors about a particular tract. Yet such information has to be taken seriously if "winning" bidders are actually to win rather than lose.

THE ANALYSIS SHOULD BE SUPPLEMENTED WITH EXPERIENCE.

One of the things oil companies have discovered offshore is that it may be useful to supplement analysis (geophysical in their case) with experience (that certain types of tracts are more likely to prove profitable than others). The logic of doing so is firmly grounded in statistical decision theory, which suggests that experience can usually be used to improve the odds of choosing the right option (see Exhibit 7.2). Theory even specifies a formal procedure, known as Bayes' Rule, for combining information freshly obtained through analysis with the prior beliefs implied by experience.[3]

Managers do not account for experience as formally as theory tells them to. They do take it seriously, though, given the extent to which they lean on it in making or influencing strategic choices.[4] Specifically, managers interpret information about strategic options in terms of their experience of what tends to work and what doesn't.

Exhibit 7.2 The Process of Choice

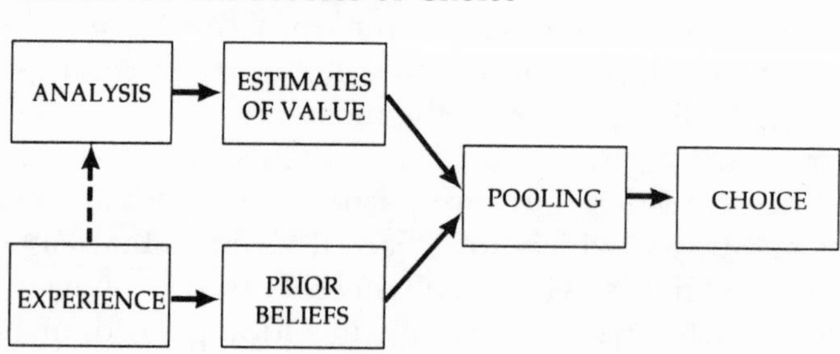

Experience directs them to look at certain options as opposed to others, colors the way those options are defined and evaluated, and is used to test the rankings that emerge from the analysis. Some of the relevant experience is purely personal or otherwise idiosyncratic. Some of it, however, while specialized to the situation at hand, draws on beliefs that are relatively generic. Three such categories of beliefs and how they influence strategic choices are discussed below.

Distinctive Competence

The *distinctive competence* of the organization (or, sometimes, business unit) is defined as whatever it can do particularly well. Implicit in this definition is the idea that each organization's distinctive competence is unique. Strategists have long believed that options consistent with the organization's (actual or intended) distinctive competence should be favored over those that are not.

The logic of using distinctive competence to help separate out worthwhile options from worthless ones has been summarized by Andrews (1980, p. 70): "Opportunism without competence is a path to fairyland." To elaborate, a successful organization is rarely all things to all people. Instead, it usually recognizes that it cannot count on beating its average competitor on *all* dimensions and therefore emphasizes doing particularly well along a particular dimension (or maybe a few). Since commitment makes it costly and disruptive to change this emphasis very frequently, strategic choices should, other things being reasonably equal, be resolved in ways consistent with it. In statistical terms, the proportion of good opportunities to bad ones is likely to be higher within the organization's zone of distinctive competence than outside it, implying the optimality of sticking to what one knows best when the analysis proves equivocal.

We need look no farther than the outer continental shelf for an application. Shell is reputed to have one of the best records in the world at hunting for oil and gas under water. Calculations by the U.S. Geological Survey confirm that it has been the top performer in the Gulf of Mexico. The man who used to run oil exploration for Shell U.S.A. attributes this success to Shell's appreciation and exploitation of its distinctive competence offshore. According to him, "We wouldn't be much good in the Permian Basin [the oil-rich onshore region around Midland, Texas], where the geology is simple and where two thousand wildcatters, all talking to each other, would put Shell, with its way of doing things, at an information disadvantage."[5] Instead, Shell has emphasized offshore exploration because most independent oilmen can't afford to explore the complex subsurface geology in the Gulf of Mexico and because Shell holds an informational advantage, thanks in part to some lucky strikes in the 1950s, over most of the oil companies that *can* pay the price of admission.

Financial Balance

A second influential belief is that the organization needs to maintain a rough balance over time between its internal supply of and demand for funds. The imposition of such a balancing constraint will influence all choices, but is likely to fall particularly heavily on strategic choices, given the magnitude of the effect they can have on funds flow.

It should be noted that the self-finance constraint is incompatible with the theory of efficient capital markets, according to which funds are always available at fair prices from external sources. Managers may nevertheless rely on such a constraint, even if they *are* interested in maximizing capital market valuations, if they have better information than investors or subordinates, or if they worry that Brealey and Myers' (1984) Second Law, cited earlier, is descriptive of their subordinates' behavior. In addition, as Donaldson and Lorsch (1983) have emphasized, managers may also be impelled toward self-finance by their sense that external capital markets are too unreliable to be depended upon.

Donaldson and Lorsch's interviews of the top managers at a dozen Fortune 500 companies underscore the emphasis that mature organizations place on financial balance. In fact, many of the companies they studied used a mathematical formula for self-sustaining growth of the sort depicted in Exhibit 7.3 to delimit the zones of financial deficit and surplus, and to avoid straying too far out into either zone, particularly the first one, in making the strategic choices that they did. This concern with financial balance is corroborated by the prevalence of portfolio planning: by 1979, 45% of the Fortune 500 companies had begun to make some use of these planning techniques, which essentially emphasize self-finance (Haspeslagh 1982).

Exhibit 7.3 The Self-Sustaining Growth Equation*

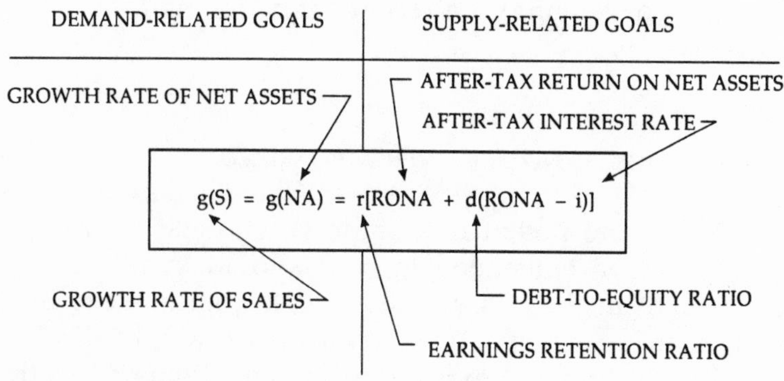

*Assumes a stable asset-to-sales ratio.

SOURCE: Donaldson and Lorsch (1983), p. 58.

Structural Context

Bower (1970, p. 71) coined the term *structural context* to refer to "the formal organization (with associated definitions of managers' jobs), the system of information and control used to measure performance of the business, and the systems used to measure and reward performance of managers." It is fairly widely believed that since these elements define the rules of the game as far as individual managers are concerned, they can be used to align their interests more closely with the organization's.

Bower's own field research at "National Products" indicates that top management relies heavily on its control of the structural context within which lower-level managers operate to influence the process whereby strategic options get defined and move toward funding. This sort of control, while indirect, is very important because lower-level managers are the ones who initiate specific options in many instances.

A somewhat different way of exploiting beliefs about contextual effects is to use them to understand how the strategic options being considered surfaced and were evaluated. Economists are very explicit about the whys and hows of debiasing the information provided by other, interested people.[6] Top managers tend to think that people are less opportunistic than economists assume but do acknowledge judging what is implicitly or explicitly being recommended partly by figuring out the story behind it. For instance, they may accord as much weight to the people championing (or, occasionally, challenging) the recommendation as to its substance (e.g., Zysman 1973).

EXPERIENCE SHOULD NOT BE OVEREMPHASIZED.

Experience has the potential to improve strategic choice because of the information embedded in it. It should therefore be given positive weight in the process of strategic choice. Keep in mind, however, that it can easily be given *too much* weight. Each of the generic ways of bringing experience to bear discussed in the last section, for example, is vulnerable to excess. The rigidity inherent in the concept of distinctive competence can inhibit adjustment to environmental changes. A self-finance constraint can screen out good as well as bad opportunities and may also invite corporate raiders. Manipulate the structural context too much and you risk hearing what your subordinate thinks you want to hear. And even the less intrusive approach of figuring out contextual biases so as to discount them can backfire. In the words of Savage (1971, p. 795),

> You might discover with experience that your expert is optimistic or pessimistic in some respect and therefore temper his judgments. Should he suspect you of this, however, you and he may well be on the escalator to perdition.

That beliefs about distinctive competence, financial balance, context and so forth had better not be used as litmus tests should come as no surprise. If distinctive competence or anything else *could* be used that way, a generic success factor would, impossibly, have been found.[7] One of the inadequacies of the success factor approach now becomes clearer. In placing its bets on prior beliefs, it essentially ignores information derived from positioning, sustainability and flexibility analysis of the choice at hand. The preceding chapters should have convinced the reader that there is too much to be learned from the analysis of strategic choices for it to be skipped.

The broader, better way of thinking about prior beliefs and analysis is that *both* must typically be given positive weight in the process of choice. Prior beliefs deserve relatively more weight when the estimation of value is mostly a matter of guesswork and when extensive, relevant experience exists. Analysis should be emphasized when the opposite conditions apply. Prior beliefs proved rather important in offshore bidding because the connection between estimated and actual values was very tenuous and because bidding was repetitive enough to let the oil companies calibrate the fractions of estimated value they bid in terms of the process averages. The typical strategic choice can perhaps be evaluated more accurately and tends to be rather more radical. My sense, therefore, is that prior beliefs should be accorded less weight in the evaluation of the typical strategic choice than of the typical tract offshore.

I should add that the process of strategic choice is significantly influenced by *how* managerial principals bring their prior beliefs to bear on the analysis their agents perform for them. Using prior beliefs only to test the rankings that emerge from the analysis avoids confusion between assumptions and observations. It also fails, however, to establish a clear sense of organizational direction. As a result, it is widely thought that principals *should* impose some structure on the process of strategic choice by prespecifying goals and (on occasion) principles that are not to be violated in pursuing them. The sorts of interventions that raise the most questions are the ones that extend beyond these limits to embrace particular means of achieving prespecified goals.[8] A forceful manager who intervenes in favor of a specific option because of strong prior beliefs about it is likely to have them played back to him or her in the analysis. This point is important enough to be worth dramatizing.

The Port Cartier Mill

Consider the pulp mill at Port Cartier, Quebec, that ITT began to build in 1971 and mothballed eight years and $600 million later.[9] The story starts in 1968 with ITT's acquisition, for $293 million, of Rayonier, the largest U.S. producer of chemical pulp. Rayonier believed that the supply of woodlands was shrinking and in 1969 began to hunt for a large tract of timber to grow on. While it detected an expansion opportunity in Quebec, where the forests were vast and the provincial government sympathetic, it decided that that opportunity should take a backseat to plans to expand at an existing site in the United States.

The plans to expand significantly in the United States were formally approved in fall 1969 at the annual review of business plans by ITT's CEO, Harold Geneen, and other top managers. Geneen is then reported to have leaned back and said, "Great! What else have you got?" In response, Rayonier's planning director described the opportunity in Quebec, characterizing the woodlands available there as "about the shape and size of Tennessee." The meeting broke up with an agreement that the viability of putting up a pulp mill in Quebec would be studied further.

A large new pulp mill in Quebec did not, on the face of it, look particularly promising. Despite low stumpage fees (governmental cutting charges), short growing seasons and extra expenses in felling trees and getting them to the mill meant that wood, the single most significant cost element, would cost half as much again in Quebec as in the southeastern United States in the early 1970s. The rough weather and poor infrastructure could be expected to add to capital as well as operating costs. So too would Geneen's support for building an unprecedentedly large plant (in keeping with the size of the woodlands) using a complex, unproven technology specialized to rayon, which accounted for less than 10% of the total demand for pulp but which Geneen and others were convinced was going to go up.

Strenuous attempts were made to find ways around these obstacles. In particular, financial analyses of the project assumed that because of rising stumpage fees, costs in the southeastern United States would eventually catch up with Quebec's, and that in spite of its complexity, the new plant would cost just 3% more per ton of capacity than the expansion under way in the United States. Despite these assumptions, the financials looked anemic: according to one source, the forecast returns on equity ranged from 10% to 13%. ITT went ahead anyway. In June 1971, it announced that a new subsidiary, Rayonier Quebec, would build a $120 million pulp mill at Port Cartier and that the Quebec and Canadian governments would contribute another $40 million toward the necessary infrastructure. The Quebec government was also to establish the 52,000 square mile Crown Forest as a source of supply for Rayonier.

Almost everything that could go wrong subsequently did. The complexities discussed earlier and labor problems combined to ensure that the mill wasn't completed till late 1974, six months behind schedule and at a cost of $250 million. Strikes recurred thereafter, compounding acute processing problems that ranged from the first step, slashing wood, to the last, wrapping rolls of pulp. The plant proved so rigid in its design that a problem in any one processing step tended to shut down everything else. Most of the output was substandard and had to be sold at a substantial discount for end uses other than rayon. And by the late 1970s, the costs of getting wood to the mill had climbed to a level 130% higher than predicted. In September 1979, ITT's board of directors voted, finally, to pull the plug on the venture.

How did such a financially shaky project survive several formal reviews at a company celebrated for managing by the numbers? The personal interest that Harold Geneen took in the project is at least part of the reason. One person who attended the review of business plans in 1969 recalls seeing Geneen huddle with a small group afterward to continue the discussion of Quebec and remembers thinking "This project is all but approved." The subsequent definition and evaluation of the Port Cartier project essentially built up a case for doing what Geneen already believed to be the right thing. As Russell Erickson, who headed Rayonier at the time, put it later, "There's no point in saying no to Mr. Geneen."

Organizations confront trade-offs between errors of omission and errors of commission.

Why did Harold Geneen think it necessary to give impetus to the proposal to build a pulp mill in Quebec? He apparently believed that the demand for rayon, and therefore for timberland, would boom but that Rayonier's management was too cautious to think big unless prodded to do so. In terms of Exhibit 7.4, Geneen was disturbed by the possibility of an error of omission. In reducing it, he increased the probability of an error of commission.

Exhibit 7.4 Possible Errors

SELECTED OPTION	APPROPRIATE OPTION: BUILD	APPROPRIATE OPTION: NOT BUILD
BUILD	CORRECT CHOICE	ERROR OF COMMISSION
NOT BUILD	ERROR OF OMISSION	CORRECT CHOICE

This way of framing what happened has several implications. It hints, first of all, at the usefulness of thinking about interventions in terms of how they affect the probabilities of particular strategic options being chosen by the organization. The *forms* intervention takes are so diverse as to resist systematic analysis. It is useful, for that reason, to be able to summarize intervention in terms of its probabilistic effects.

Second, intervention will, if effective, tend to alter the trade-off that the organization strikes between errors of omission and of commission. In the context of Exhibit 7.4, for instance, interventions affect the probability that the organization will build rather than not. Interventions that operate to increase the probability of building also increase the possibility of an error of commission. Interventions that have the opposite effect increase the possibility of an error of omission. Interventions that don't affect the probabilities can, it was argued above, be ignored.

Infallibility supplies the only exception to the otherwise obligatory trade-off between errors of omission and of commission. In terms of Exhibit 7.4, an organization that always chooses correctly can count on landing in one of the two boxes on the principal (northwest-southeast) diagonal. Otherwise, however, it must cope with the possibility of both types of error. It usually isn't sensible to try to stamp out either type of error, even though errors of omission could be eliminated by accepting all commitment proposals and errors of commission by accepting none at all. Instead, it usually makes sense to try to strike an interior trade-off between the two by accepting positive levels of both.

Exhibit 7.5 traces the trade-off between errors of omission and commission. Random judgments that ignore the information embedded in experience and obtained from analysis lead to a total probability of error of one that is split between errors of omission and commission in proportion to the ratio of rejected-to-accepted commitment proposals. While enlightened judgments intersect both axes at the same places as do random ones, they otherwise shift the frontier of what is possible in the right direction, inward. Extra information will permit it to be pushed even farther in. Unfortunately, the point of maximum bliss, associated with zero error and so marked in the exhibit, is usually unattainable.

If the first-best outcome cannot be attained, what spot on the second-best frontier should the organization strive for? Intuition suggests and statistical theory confirms that it makes sense to operate

Exhibit 7.5 The Probabilities of Error

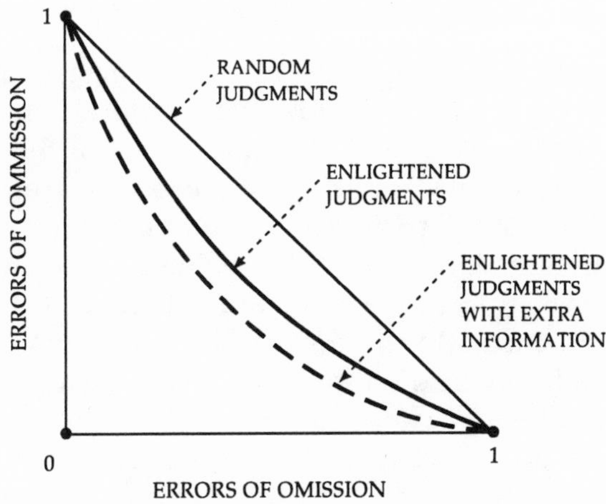

comparatively far up the frontier when errors of commission are inexpensive compared to errors of omission, and comparatively far down when the reverse is true. In other words, when an error of a particular type is particularly costly, it makes sense to go out of one's way to avoid it, even though that somewhat increases the costs of the other type of error.

Statistical theory permits even greater precision. It implies that the second-best optimum is given by the point of tangency between the frontier and a straight line whose slope is the reciprocal of the ratio of the losses expected from the two types of error. This characterization confirms that the last chapter was on the right track in emphasizing the maximization of expected gains: the minimization of expected losses implicit in the tangency condition amounts to the same thing, except that it is supposed to be based on information that encompasses experience as well as analysis. One possible way of integrating the two is suggested by the crypton case discussed in the last chapter. The committee in charge of new ventures took the conditional payoffs implied by the analysis of the success and failure scenarios as given, and compared the implied break-even probability of success with prior beliefs about the likelihood that success would in fact be achieved. It thereby avoided the bother of aggregating conditional expectations based on the analysis into unconditional ones and then disaggregating them again so as to take prior beliefs into account.

DIFFERENT ORGANIZATIONAL ARRANGEMENTS TEND TO LEAD TO DIFFERENT MIXES OF ERROR.

Failure to recognize and manage the trade-off between errors of omission and of commission—what is sometimes referred to as an error of the third type—wouldn't be *too* serious if the organization could count on an excess of caution in some instances and a deficit in others to cancel out. Unfortunately, indivisibilities in the process whereby the organization identifies, evaluates and chooses among strategic options imply a positive rather than zero correlation of errors from one choice to the next (unless, of course, the process has changed radically in the interim or is short circuited). The tendency toward extremes that results can be highlighted by identifying two polar types of organizations on the basis of their propensities to commit the two types of error.

Type I organizations are less likely to accept bad commitment opportunities but more likely to pass up good ones. The structure of such organizations tends to be characterized by relatively many layers of hierarchy and monolithic authority relationships. Hierarchical structures of this sort correspond to a number of information-processing devices or screens arrayed in series, each of which must approve a commitment opportunity for it to be accepted. Intuitively, as the number of screens increases, the probability of acceptance goes down, reducing the incidence of errors of commission but increasing the incidence of errors of omission.[10] Type I organizations are likely to lean on consistency constraints, such as the concept of distinctive competence and centralized budgets, in making their strategic choices, and to emphasize efficiency in subordinate choices.

Type II organizations tend to be less conservative than Type I organizations: they are more likely to accept bad commitment opportunities but less likely to pass up good ones. This makes them reverse images of Type I organizations. Type II structure is more horizontal and less vertical: it incorporates more teamwork and less hierarchy and can be viewed as an array of information-processing devices that are placed in parallel rather than series and that therefore presuppose extensive coordination. Such organizations are less likely to emphasize consistency constraints in making their strategic choices, and more likely to emphasize adjustment (or dynamic efficiency) than static efficiency in subordinate choices. This last difference often leads Type II organizations toward output-based monitoring instead of the direct monitoring of inputs: examples include an emphasis on variety (which attracts customers) instead of run length (which minimizes the costs of producing any given amount), on speed in delivering new products to customers rather than the costs of doing so, and on investment in flexible factors of production if they don't cost "too" much more than specialized ones for the intended set of product applications.

While these are composite pictures, they do suggest a comparative advantage for Type I organizations in stable environments and for Type II organizations in turbulent ones. This is consistent with the fundamental dogma of modern organization theory: that the optimal structure of organizations depends on the environments they have to relate to and how they chose to do so. In spite of this contingency, Type II organizational arrangements are the ones that everybody seems to be excited about. It will be useful to illustrate this excitement before assessing it.

General Electric

My example concerns General Electric (GE), which has long been acclaimed as an organizational pioneer and which began trying, in the early 1980s, to transform itself into a Type II organization. A GE executive has provided a concise summary of the earlier history.[11]

> We came out of World War II a finely honed, centralized, functionally organized company. When we decentralized in the early fifties, we did so with a vengeance, almost to the point of acting like a holding company. Setting up the SBUs [Strategic Business Units] in 1970 was a recognition that we had gone too far, and that the strategic direction of the company should be made from the top to some extent. The sector executives in 1977 helped move the pendulum a little further in that direction.

John F. Welch, Jr., took over as GE's Chief Executive Officer (CEO) on April 1, 1981, with a burning conviction that the company needed to be reorganized. Eight years later, at GE's annual meeting, he summarized the company's direction since he had taken the helm in a major speech titled, "Speed, Simplicity, Self-Confidence: Keys to Leading in the '90s." The excerpts from the speech that are reproduced in Exhibit 7.6 should make it clear that Welch's emphasis on the three Ss reflects his belief that the company his predecessor passed on to him needed to become more Type II, to

Exhibit 7.6 John Welch on General Electric

We found in the '80s that speed increases in an organization as control decreases. We had constructed over the years a management apparatus that was right for its times, the toast of the business schools. Divisions, strategic business units, groups, sectors, all were designed to make meticulous, calculated decisions and move them smoothly forward and upward. This system produced highly polished work. It was right for the '70s. . . a growing handicap in the early '80s. . . and it would have been a ticket to the boneyard in the '90s. So we got rid of it.. . .

We found in the '80s that becoming faster is tied to becoming simpler. Our businesses, most with tens of thousands of employees, will not respond to visions that have sub-paragraphs and footnotes.. . . In the '90s cultures like that will produce sophisticated decisions loaded with nuance and complexity that arrive at the station long after the train has gone.. . . we believe the nexus between simplicity and speed is so important, so critical to winning in the '90s that we have embarked upon a company-wide crusade we call "Work-out".. . .

But just as surely as speed flows from simplicity, simplicity is grounded in self-confidence. Self-confidence does not grow in someone who is just another appendage on the bureaucracy. . . whose authority rests on little more than a title. Bureaucracy is terrified by speed and hates simplicity. It fosters defensiveness, intrigue, sometimes meanness. Those who are trapped in it are afraid to share, can't be passionate and—in the '90s—won't win.

—Speech, April 26,1989

commit fewer errors of omission, even if that entailed an increase in errors of commission.

Welch can point to some specific successes as a result of this change in direction. He cited one in an interview published in the *Harvard Business Review* under the same title as his speech (Tichy and Charan 1989, pp. 115–116):

> Take the deal with Thomson, where we swapped our consumer electronics business for their medical equipment business. We were presented with an opportunity, a great solution to a serious strategic problem, and we were able to act quickly. We didn't need to go back to headquarters for a strategic analysis and a bunch of reports. Conceptually, it took us about 30 minutes to decide that the deal made sense and then a meeting of maybe two hours with the Thomson people to work out the basic terms. We signed a letter of intent in five days.

Rough financial analysis of this deal (based on the framework described in this book) suggests that it was worth several hundred million dollars to General Electric.

The decrease in errors of omission seems to have been accompanied, however, by an increase in errors of commission. The refrigerator business offers an instance of the latter.[12] Facing a severe cost disadvantage in compressors, which are the most expensive part of refrigerators, GE decided that it would switch to a simpler, rotary design that would allow it to narrow and perhaps even eliminate its disadvantage. This option also embodied speed in the sense that the switch was supposed to happen all at once, and self-confidence in that a drastic design change would be involved and mass production at unprecedented precision would be required to make it work. Welch personally approved the move even though the betting was that he wouldn't.

The first rotary compressors began rolling out of a new factory supposed to showcase GE's advanced manufacturing skills in early 1986. By early 1988, GE had discovered that the larger units had a design flaw that made some of them fail in the field. In order to safeguard its reputation in one of its core businesses, GE has had to engage in an extensive program to replace them preventively instead of just replacing the few that do break down. The total cost of the repairs alone has been pegged at several hundreds of millions of dollars. Without the emphasis on the three Ss, it is more likely that GE would either have sourced its compressors or introduced the new technology far more gradually and at far less of a cost.

Lessons

The most obvious lesson from the GE case is that there *will* be failures—that the point marked "0" in Exhibit 7.5 cannot be attained. That seems, in turn, to suggest several less obvious lessons.

First, the way the organization handles its failures may be as (or even more) important as how it rewards success.[13] GE has grasped this point if the Halarc story is any guide.[14] Halarc was GE's attempt to miniaturize a highly complicated light source so as to develop a bulb for the consumer market that could shine like a regular 150-watt bulb, last five times longer and use one-third as much electricity. GE decided to go ahead with Halarc in

1979 because while the risk of failure was high—the design was complex and its cost meant that the new bulb would have to be priced relatively high (at $10) in the price-sensitive consumer market—it seemed to be worth incurring in light of the predicted life-cycle energy cost savings to the customer of $40-75 per bulb. GE shelved the project four years later, after test market failure. What is more remarkable is the attention that it reportedly paid to rewarding the engineers and planners involved, in ways that ranged from award parties, dinners and ceremonies for the team members after their product was shelved to the assurance that good job assignments were waiting for them. Given Halarc's visibility within the company, the post-failure treatment of the project team seemed the ideal occasion to convince employees that GE was serious about passing up fewer opportunities, i.e., becoming more of a Type II organization.

Second, given how GE was organized in the early 1980s and how its environment was changing around it, it probably *did* make sense for the company to try to become more Type II. The same may be true for many other large U.S. companies, for two complementary reasons. A variety of technological changes—the development of computer networks and electronic data transmission systems, the emergence of computer-aided design and the introduction of robots and other programmable production equipment—may have expanded the range of environments in which "informated" Type II organizations have an advantage (Milgrom and Roberts 1990). And the globalization of competition may have reinforced this tendency. In particular, it has been suggested that Japanese competitors, having emerged from a more turbulent domestic environment, may have forced a new set of trade-offs on U.S. companies accustomed to stability and organized on the basis of that premise (Henderson 1990). It is unlikely, though, that these changes have been sweeping enough to make Type II organizations universally better than Type I organizations.

Third, while reorganizing to become more effective may (sometimes) be necessary, it is no panacea, even though Welch and many other top managers often assert that it is. Reconsider the historical record at GE, which was summarized in a quotation earlier in this section. GE came out of World War II a Type I organization, became more of a Type II organization in the 1950s, reverted to Type I in the 1970s, and swung back toward Type II in the early 1980s. Each swing of the pendulum was closely associated with a specific CEO. Similar tendencies toward extremes have been observed at other large companies by Pascale (1990) and Miller (1990).[15] Such tendencies discourage the idea that reorganization is *the* solution to business problems. I suspect, as Miller seems to, that these costly tendencies often stem from the overemphasis of formulas that have succeeded in the past. That is one of the reasons I was so hard on success factors in chapter 1.

Finally, and most importantly, there is no substitute for the *analysis* of commitment-intensive or strategic choices. Reconsider GE's switch to rotary compressors. It is hard to tell exactly how much weight was attached to the prior beliefs embodied in the three Ss, as opposed to analysis, in making that choice. But if the three Ss *were* used to overrule strong analytic arguments against the switch, that was poor judgment for reasons that have nothing to do with the fact that it led to a bad outcome.

Summary

Care in conducting the sorts of analysis discussed in this book, while desirable, will not eradicate the possibility of error. Some of that error can be eliminated by supplementing analysis with experience. Some of it, however, is irreducible and forces the organization to trade off errors of omission (passing up too many good commitments) and errors of commission (making too many bad ones). While organizational arrangements that lead to fewer errors of omission seem to be fashionable in the early 1990s, they do have the awkward effect of increasing the incidence of errors of commission. In the terminology of chapter 1, organizing a particular way is no more of a success as a success factor than anything else. The important thing is to figure out which choices are critical and to devote extra attention to trying to get them right.

Notes

CHAPTER 1
Strategy: The Failure of Success Factors

1. Barnard actually borrowed the idea of the strategic factor, the potash example and all, from the economist John Commons (1934).
2. The broadest survey as of this writing is Henry Mintzberg's (1990). Mintzberg does not, however, make the connection between prevalent strategic prescriptions and success factors. For that, see Raphael Amit and Paul Schoemaker (1990).
3. Wal-Mart's situation in 1984 is described in considerably more detail by Pankaj Ghemawat (1986a).
4. Nancy Cartwright (1983) discusses at considerable length why causal explanations are logically necessary in this context, and why they can be correct only if the processes they describe really take place.
5. For a book-length exposition, consult Michael Hannan and John Freeman's *Organizational Ecology* (1989).
6. Frank Knight's *Risk, Uncertainty, and Profit* (1921) is the classic account.
7. Consult, for instance, Richard Caves, Bradley Gale and Michael Porter's "Interfirm Profitability Differences: Comment" (1977).

CHAPTER 2
Commitment: The Persistence of Strategies

1. The concept of punctuated equilibria originated in evolutionary biology. Niles Eldredge and Stephen Gould's "Punctuated Equilibria: An Alternative to Phyletic Gradualism" (1972) is the seminal article.

2. I have omitted the mathematics. Readers with an appetite for it may wish to consult Lionel McKenzie (1960) on the continuity-related properties of matrices of the "dominant diagonal" type.
3. Richard Caves (1980) has emphasized the role sticky factors have played in earlier works on strategy.
4. Consult, for instance, Martin Weitzman (1983).
5. This quotation is taken from Patrick Wright's *On a Clear Day You Can See General Motors* (1979, p. 100).
6. Oliver Williamson (1975, pp. 121–122) has elaborated the organizational economics of inertia.
7. David Kreps and Michael Spence's early essay, "Modeling the Role of History in Industrial Organization and Competition" (1984), is still the best overview of the theoretical literature on committed competition. The connections with the literature on strategy have been articulated by Richard Caves (1984).
8. This is the answer to the question of generality that I raised in regard to success factors: why aren't monopoly profits totally dissipated by competition to become the monopolist, etc.? For additional discussion, see my 1991 paper, "The Economic Analysis of Factor *and* Product Market Imperfections."
9. Regulated industries supply the sole exception to this rule: they can exhibit sustained performance differentials even in the absence of commitment opportunities. The importance of this exception is qualified by the fact that if an industry did not offer any commitment opportunities, there would be no real reason to regulate it in the first place. The rationale for airline deregulation, which I discuss next, is relevant in this regard.
10. The standard reference on contestability theory is William Baumol, John Panzar and Robert Willig's *Contestable Markets and the Theory of Industry Structure* (1982). While Baumol, Panzar and Willig's definition of perfect contestability differs formally from the one implied here, the theorems they work out essentially rest on the assumption of zero commitment.
11. For a more detailed discussion, consult Michael Levine's "Airline Competition in Deregulated Markets" (1987).
12. I owe the distinction between strategizing and economizing to Oliver Williamson (1990), who associates the former with a power-based perspective on strategy, and the latter with an efficiency-based perspective. Researchers have recently identified several factor attributes that should be associated positively with the scope for strategizing: the complexity of the factor (Paul Schoemaker 1990), lags in adjusting it (e.g., Kenneth Judd 1990) and the ability to play escalation games with it (John Sutton 1991). Capacity scores relatively low on all three attributes in many instances; knowledge tends to score higher. The hypothesis that capac-

ity-dominated industries offer relatively few degrees of strategic freedom draws some empirical support from my 1986 and 1989 papers with Richard Caves.

13. Sectors are defined at the 2-digit Standard Industrial Classification (SIC) level, and industries at the 4-digit level. The cutoff points for the top one-third of industries are physical capital stocks booked at 70% of value added, advertising expenses equal to 2.8% of value added, and R&D expenses equal to 1.7% of value added.
14. That is why some recent books, such as Ilya Prigogine and Isabelle Stengers' *Order Out of Chaos* (1984), propose irreversibility as an integrative theme for all of the natural and social sciences.

Chapter 3
Choice: Making Commitments

1. The problem of prediction posed by nonlinearities is discussed at greater length by David Berlinski (1976), pp. 112–155.
2. For more detailed mappings of the literature that confirm this polarization, consult chapter 11 of Amitai Etzioni's *The Active Society* (1968) or chapter 1 of David Bell, Howard Raiffa and Amos Tversky's coedited volume, *Decision Making* (1988).
3. Consult, for instance, Claude Henry (1974) and Jeffrey Banks, John Ledyard and David Porter (1989).
4. Also see Alfred Chandler (1990).
5. Also see Michael Tushman, William Newman and Elaine Romanelli (1987).
6. There is also an analogy between the two feedback loops required for self-stabilization and "double-loop" learning of the sort lauded by Chris Argyris and Donald Schon (1978). The next paragraph makes it clear, however, that the analogy isn't entirely apt.
7. I should emphasize that I am talking about *market* games instead of the *nonmarket* games, typically involving more coordination, that tend to be encountered within organizational or inter-organizational coalitions. Strategic complementarity seems to be quite frequent in the context of coalitions but may be rarer in the context of competitive market games: the applied literature on the latter (e.g., Michael Porter 1985) has emphasized the possibility of playing so aggressively as to force rivals to back down.

Chapter 4
Positioning: Creating Value

1. Classical decision theory attempts to identify the best option on the basis of predictions about what the other "players" will do. Game

theory tries, in addition, to account for the dependence of their actions on the option actually pursued. The next chapter uses a "reduced-form" version of game theory to tackle the task of predicting competitor reactions.

2. No exception is supposed to be made for choices about diversification, even though their logic is fundamentally cross-market. See Michael Porter's "From Competitive Advantage to Corporate Strategy" (1987).
3. Consult, for instance, Derek Abell's *Defining the Business* (1980) or Michael Porter's *Competitive Strategy* (1980).
4. The presumption in favor of working with the organization's existing channels of information has been elaborated by Kenneth Arrow (1974).
5. This last condition is coterminous with the one previous to it: costs should be separated into discrete categories only if the factor differentials implicit in the options being considered are likely to influence them in quite different ways.
6. Consult, for instance, Joe Bain (1956) on the differences that shield product market incumbents from would-be entrants and Richard Caves and Pankaj Ghemawat (1989) on the differences that account for variations in the performance of large, directly competitive incumbents.
7. The somewhat abstract labels of "K" and "r" that population ecologists use to describe alternate generic strategies reflect the notation normally used in biological models to describe population dynamics.
8. The first three conditions are synthesized by Pankaj Ghemawat and Michael Spence (1986), and the fourth one by Avner Shaked and John Sutton (1987).
9. In the jargon of decision theory, Exhibit 4.2 is an *influence diagram,* a decision tree with time stripped out of it. Such timelessness is supposed to make influence diagrams a particularly transparent way of eliciting, representing and communicating knowledge. See Ronald Howard (1988).
10. Tom Copeland, Tim Koller and Jack Murrin's *Valuation* (1990) treats the determination of the appropriate discount rate and other finance-related issues in a relatively nontechnical way.
11. When the effects of strategic options *aren't* open-ended, the time-depth of the analysis should not exceed the economic life of the differential factors associated with different commitment options.
12. The discussion that follows is based on an excellent case description-cum-analysis by John Wells (1982). Some of the data have been simplified or disguised.
13. BUR membrane, in keeping with its name, is built up with layers of hot asphalt into a multidecker sandwich on the roof. Single-ply membrane, in contrast, is stretched over the roof, without any hot asphalt,

in one layer and then either attached to it or held in place by rocks placed on top (ballast).

14. Ballastability was not an issue with BUR membrane because hot asphalt glued it to the roof.
15. Trended out to 1990, which was used as the horizon for some computer modeling, differences in their forecast inflation rates implied a better than 3-to-1 edge for modified bitumen over EPDM.

Chapter 5
Sustainability: Claiming Value

1. Edward Zajac and Max Bazerman's "Blind Spots in Industry and Competitor Analysis" (1991) discusses some of the possible reasons for this bias.
2. Studies using different performance measures or time periods have come up with qualitatively similar results.
3. According to a formula concocted by a consulting firm that specializes in such matters, a long-run margin three-and-a-half percentage points greater than the cost of capital implies, for an "average" business whose volume is growing at the very moderate rate of 2% to 3%, an investment benefit-to-cost ratio of about 250%. Slightly higher growth assumptions are supposed to expand this already sizeable premium significantly.
4. My 1986 article in the *Harvard Business Review* discusses the evidence on imitation in more detail. It also contains specific citations.
5. Game-theoretic equilibrium concepts can, in principle, be employed to predict the responses of rational competitors. But opinions about their predictive efficacy vary. Contrast, for instance, companion essays by Franklin Fisher (1989) and Carl Shapiro (1989).
6. This typology is based on earlier ones by Pankaj Ghemawat (1986b) and by Richard Rumelt (1987). Ingemar Dierickx and Karel Cool (1989) take a complementary approach—one that focuses on factor accumulation processes instead of the stocks that result.
7. More details can be found in my 1991 paper, "Market Incumbency and Technological Inertia."
8. The description here draws, in part, on Michael Porter's case study, "The NFL vs. the USFL" (1986).
9. Richard Caves and David Barton (1990) survey and make a significant contribution to the evidence on the existence and determinants of slack.
10. Oliver Williamson (1985, especially chap. 6) provides a particularly interesting discussion of the ineradicable limits to organizational effi-

ciency. The final section of the final chapter of this book is also relevant: it suggests that organizations tend to face a trade-off between the (static) efficiency of the factors they choose to deploy and the ability to change those deployments in response to environmental changes.

11. For a relatively balanced discussion, consult Douglas Smith and Robert Alexander's *Fumbling the Future* (1988), particularly chapter 1.
12. Additional details appear in my 1984 paper, "Capacity Expansion in the Titanium Dioxide Industry."

Chapter 6
Flexibility: The Value of Recourse

1. Consult, for instance, Kenneth Judd's "Credible Spatial Preemption" (1985).
2. The data on capacity announcements are based on a private communication from Marvin Lieberman. Hugh Davidson (1976) and Edwin Mansfield (1981) discuss, respectively, the revision rates associated with new brands and with R&D programs.
3. Consult, for instance, Thomas Klammer and Michael Walker's "The Continuing Increase in the Use of Sophisticated Capital Budgeting Techniques" (1984).
4. Carl Kester's "Today's Options for Tomorrow's Growth" (1984) discusses this point in more detail.
5. Many of the stylized facts in this subsection are drawn from a detailed description of the venture capital industry by William Sahlman (1991).
6. The number of stages or options can be increased without affecting the principles developed in this chapter. Consult Robert Jones and David Ostroy's "Flexibility and Uncertainty" (1984) for a formal proof.
7. Robert Libby and Peter Fishburn (1977) survey the psychological research on this point.
8. Refer, for instance, to Lawrence Schall, Gary Sundem and William Geijsbeek's "Survey and Analysis of Capital Budgeting Methods" (1978) and Thomas Klammer and Michael Walker's "The Continuing Increase in the Use of Sophisticated Capital Budgeting Techniques" (1984).
9. This bias has been documented in numerous psychological studies. See, for instance, Sarah Lichtenstein, Baruch Fischoff and Lawrence Phillips' "Calibration of Probabilities: The State of the Art" (1977).
10. Consult, for instance, Paul Schoemaker (1991).
11. See, for instance, David M. Schweiger and William R. Sandberg (1989).
12. Some of the reasons it may be easier to form conditional expectations than unconditional ones are discussed by Fischer Black (1988).

13. To make matters worse, adjustability is often confused with *true* (as defined here) flexibility. For more discussion of the distinction between the two, consult Burton Klein's *Prices, Wages and Business Cycles* (1984).
14. While the failure scenario could have held sales potential to the (low) level already achieved, this assumption seemed too extreme to the team to be remotely plausible. Sales *were* increasing fairly quickly at the time of the analysis.
15. This characterization is borrowed from Paul Schoemaker (1991).
16. The fact that the costs were underestimated probably reflects a focus on success scenarios.
17. This description of Time's misadventure is largely based on Christopher Byron's *The Fanciest Dive* (1986).
18. Consult, for instance, Barry Staw (1981) who has labeled this phenomenon "escalating commitment," although the explanation he seems to have in mind is the sunk cost fallacy. The discussion of organizational inertia in chapter 2 should have made it clear that the noneconomic sources of commitment to broad courses of action are potentially much more diverse.

Chapter 7
Judgment: Coping with Error

1. Consult Otis Gilley, Gordon Karels and Robert Leone (1986) and Richard Engelbrecht-Wiggans, Elmer Dougherty and John Lohrenz (1986).
2. Consult Kenneth Hendricks and Robert H. Porter (1988).
3. Robert Schlaifer's *Probability and Statistics for Business Decisions* (1959) contains a clear discussion.
4. See, for instance, Gordon Donaldson and Jay Lorsch's *Decision Making at the Top* (1983).
5. This quotation is drawn from Robert Waterman's *The Renewal Factor* (1987), p. 29.
6. See, for instance, Paul Milgrom and John Roberts' "Relying on the Information of Interested Parties" (1986).
7. Note, in this regard, the affinity between distinctive competence and some of the success factors discussed in chapter 1.
8. See, for instance, Richard Hackman's "The Psychology of Self-Management in Organizations" (1986).
9. The description of the Port Cartier mill is based, in large part, on Carol Loomis' article in *Fortune*, "How I.T.T. Got Lost in a Big Bad Forest" (1979).
10. For a formalization of the effects of internal organization on the relative incidence of the two types of errors, consult Raaj Kumar Sah and

Joseph Stiglitz's "The Architecture of Economic Systems: Hierarchies and Polyarchies" (1986).

11. This quote is taken from Richard F. Vancil (1981).
12. I draw here principally on an upbeat account by Ira Magaziner and Mark Patinkin, "Cold Competition: GE Wages the Refrigerator War" (1989).
13. The treatment of failures may have more of an impact on managerial incentives because of the widely reported tendency toward loss-aversion. See Daniel Kahneman and Dan Lovallo (1990).
14. The Halarc story was initially reported in GE's internal magazine and reprinted in a Harvard Business School case by Francis Aguilar, Richard Hamermesh and Caroline Brainard (1985).
15. Classical Greek philosophers even had a word for such tendencies toward extremes: *enantiodromia*. See Richard Pascale (1990, p. 174).

References

Abell, Derek F. 1980. *Defining the Business.* Englewood Cliffs, N.J.: Prentice-Hall.

Aguilar, Francis, J., Richard G. Hamermesh, and Caroline Brainard. 1985. "General Electric: 1984." Intercollegiate Case Clearinghouse No. 9–385–315, Harvard Business School.

Aharoni, Yair. 1966. *The Foreign Investment Decision Process.* Boston: Division of Research, Graduate School of Business Administration, Harvard University.

Ainslie, George. 1975. "Specious Reward: A Behavioral Theory of Impulsiveness and Impulse Control." *Psychological Bulletin,* Vol. 82, No. 4 (July): 463–496.

Alchian, Armen A., and Susan Woodward. 1988. "The Firm Is Dead: Long Live the Firm." *Journal of Economic Literature,* Vol. 26, No. 1 (March): 65–79.

Amit, Raphael, and Paul J. Schoemaker. 1990. "Key Success Factors: Their Foundation and Application." Mimeo, University of British Columbia (July).

Andrews, Kenneth R. 1980. *The Concept of Corporate Strategy.* Homewood, Ill.: Richard D. Irwin.

Argyris, Chris, and Donald A. Schon. 1978. *Organizational Learning: A Theory of Action Perspective.* Reading, Mass.: Addison-Wesley.

Arrow, Kenneth J. 1964. "Optimal Capital Policy, the Cost of Capital, and Myopic Decision Rules." *Annals of the Institute of Statistics and Mathematics, Tokyo,* Vol. 16: 21–30.

———. 1968. "Optimal Capital Policy with Irreversible Investment." In

J. N. Wolfe, ed., *Value, Capital, and Growth*. Edinburgh: Edinburgh University Press.

———. 1974. *The Limits of Organization*. New York: Norton.

Ashby, W. Ross. 1956. *Design for a Brain*. New York: John Wiley.

Bain, Joe S. 1956. *Barriers to New Competition*. Cambridge, Mass.: Harvard University Press.

Baldwin, Carliss Y., and Kim B. Clark. 1990. "Capabilities, Time Horizons and Investment: New Perspectives on Capital Budgeting." Mimeo, Harvard Business School (December).

Bales, Carter F., P. C. Chatterjee, Donald J. Gogel, and Anupam P. Puri. 1980. "Competitive Cost Analysis." McKinsey Staff Paper (January).

Ball, Ben C., Jr. 1987. "The Mysterious Disappearance of Retained Earnings." *Harvard Business Review*, Vol. 65, No. 4 (July–August): 56–63.

Banks, Jeffrey S., John O. Ledyard, and David P. Porter. 1989. "Allocating Uncertain and Unresponsive Resources: An Experimental Approach." *Rand Journal of Economics*, Vol. 20, No. 1 (Spring): 1–25.

Barnard, Chester I. 1938. *The Functions of the Executive*. Cambridge, Mass.: Harvard University Press.

Baumol, William J., John C. Panzar, and Robert D. Willig. 1982. *Contestable Markets and the Theory of Industry Structure*. New York: Harcourt Brace Jovanovich.

Bell, David E., Howard Raiffa, and Amos Tversky, eds. 1988. *Decision Making: Descriptive, Normative and Prescriptive Interactions*. Cambridge: Cambridge University Press.

Berlinski, David. 1976. *On Systems Analysis*. Cambridge, Mass.: MIT Press.

Black, Fischer. 1988. "A Simple Discounting Rule." *Financial Management*, Vol. 17, No. 2 (Summer): 7–11.

Bonoma, Thomas V. 1981. "Market Success Can Breed 'Marketing Inertia.'" *Harvard Business Review*, Vol. 59, No. 5 (September–October): 115–121.

Boston Consulting Group. 1975. *Strategy Alternatives for the British Motorcycle Industry*. London: Her Majesty's Stationery Office.

Bower, Joseph L. 1970. *Managing the Resource Allocation Process*. Boston: Division of Research, Graduate School of Business Administration, Harvard University.

Bradburd, Ralph M., and Richard E. Caves. 1982. "A Closer Look at the Effect of Market Growth on Industries' Profits." *Review of Economics and Statistics*, Vol. 64, No. 4 (November): 635–645.

Brealey, Richard A., and Stewart C. Myers. 1984. *Principles of Corporate Finance*. New York: McGraw-Hill.

Bresnahan, Timothy F. 1986. "The Transition to Competition in the Plain Paper Copier Market." Federal Trade Commission, Washington, D.C.

Bulow, Jeremy I., John D. Geanakoplos, and Paul D. Klemperer. 1985. "Multimarket Oligopoly: Strategic Substitutes and Complements." *Journal of Political Economy,* Vol. 93, No. 3 (June): 488–511.

Byron, Christopher. 1986. *The Fanciest Dive.* New York: New American Library.

Capen, E. C., R. V. Clapp, and W. M. Campbell. 1971. "Competitive Bidding in High-Risk Situations." *Journal of Petroleum Technology,* Vol. 23 (June): 641–653.

Cartwright, Nancy. 1983. *How the Laws of Physics Lie.* Oxford: Clarendon Press.

Caves, Richard E. 1980. "Industrial Organization, Corporate Strategy and Structure." *Journal of Economic Literature,* Vol. 18, No. 1 (March): 64–92.

———. 1984. "Economic Analysis and the Quest for Competitive Advantage." *American Economic Review,* Vol. 74, No. 2 (May): 127–132.

Caves, Richard E., and David R. Barton. 1990. *Efficiency in U.S. Manufacturing Industries.* Cambridge, Mass.: MIT Press.

Caves, Richard E., Michael Fortunato, and Pankaj Ghemawat. 1984. "The Decline of Dominant Firms, 1905–1929." *Quarterly Journal of Economics,* Vol. 99, No. 3 (August): 523–546.

Caves, Richard E., Bradley T. Gale, and Michael E. Porter. 1977. "Interfirm Profitability Differences: Comment." *Quarterly Journal of Economics,* Vol. 91, No. 4 (November): 667–675.

Caves, Richard E., and Pankaj Ghemawat. 1989. "Identifying Mobility Barriers." Working Paper No. 89–017, Harvard Business School (April).

Chandler, Alfred D., Jr. 1990. *Scale and Scope: The Dynamics of Industrial Capitalism.* Cambridge, Mass.: Belknap Press of Harvard University Press.

Clausewitz, Carl von. 1833. *On War.* Ed. and trans. Michael Howard and Peter Paret. Princeton: Princeton University Press (1984).

Cohen, Wesley M., and Richard C. Levin. 1989. "Empirical Studies of Innovation and Market Structure." In R. Schmalensee and R. D. Willig, eds., *Handbook of Industrial Organization,* Vol. 2. Amsterdam: North-Holland.

Collis, David J. 1986. "The Value Added Structure and Competition within Industries." Unpublished Ph.D. dissertation, Harvard University.

———. 1990. "Commitment Opportunities and the Structure-Conduct-Performance Paradigm." Mimeo, Harvard Business School (June).

Commons, John R. 1934. *Institutional Economics.* New York: MacMillan.

Copeland, Tom, Tim Koller, and Jack Murrin. 1990. *Valuation.* New York: John Wiley.

Davidson, J. Hugh. 1976. "Why Most New Consumer Brands Fail." *Harvard Business Review,* Vol. 54, No. 2 (March–April): 117–122.

Deal, Terrence E., and Allen A. Kennedy. 1982. *Corporate Cultures.* Reading, Mass.: Addison-Wesley.

Dierickx, Ingemar, and Karel Cool. 1989. "Asset Stock Accumulation and Sustainability of Competitive Advantage." *Management Science,* Vol. 35, No. 12 (December): 1504–1514.

Donaldson, Gordon. 1989. "The Corporate Restructuring Cycle." Mimeo, Harvard Business School.

Donaldson, Gordon, and Jay W. Lorsch. 1983. *Decision Making at the Top.* New York: Basic Books.

Duncan, Robert B. 1972. "Characteristics of Organizational Environments and Perceived Environmental Uncertainty." *Administrative Science Quarterly,* Vol. 17, No. 3 (September): 313–327.

Eldredge, Niles, and Stephen J. Gould. 1972. "Punctuated Equilibria: An Alternative to Phyletic Gradualism." In T. J. M. Schopf, ed., *Models in Paleobiology.* San Francisco: Freeman Cooper.

Engelbrecht-Wiggans, Richard, Elmer L. Dougherty, and John Lohrenz. 1986. "A Model for the Distribution of the Number of Bids on Federal Offshore Oil Leases." *Management Science,* Vol. 32, No. 9 (September): 1087–1094.

Etzioni, Amitai. 1968. *The Active Society: A Theory of Societal and Political Processes.* New York: Free Press.

———. 1988. *The Moral Dimension: Toward a New Economics.* New York: Free Press.

Fisher, Franklin M. 1989. "Games Economists Play: A Noncooperative View." *RAND Journal of Economics,* Vol. 20, No. 1 (Spring): 113–124.

Galsworthy, John. 1932. *The Flowering Wilderness.* New York: Scribner's.

Ghemawat, Pankaj. 1984. "Capacity Expansion in the Titanium Dioxide Industry." *Journal of Industrial Economics,* Vol. 33, No. 2 (December): 145–163.

———. 1986a. "Wal-Mart Stores' Discount Operations." Intercollegiate Case Clearinghouse No. 9-387-018.

———. 1986b. "Sustainable Advantage." *Harvard Business Review,* Vol. 64, No. 5 (September–October): 53–58.

———. 1987. "Investment in Lumpy Capacity." *Journal of Economic Behavior and Organization,* Vol. 8, No. 2 (June): 265–277.

———. 1991a. "The Economic Analysis of Factor *and* Product Market Imperfections." Mimeo, Harvard Business School (January).

———. 1991b. "Market Incumbency and Technological Inertia." *Marketing Science,* Vol. 10, No. 2 (Spring), forthcoming.

Ghemawat, Pankaj, and Richard E. Caves. 1986. "Capital Commitment and Profitability: An Empirical Investigation." *Oxford Economic Papers,* Vol. 38, Supplement (November): 94–110.

Ghemawat, Pankaj, and A. Michael Spence. 1986. "Modeling Global Competition." In M. E. Porter, ed., *Competition in Global Industries.* Boston: Harvard Business School Press.

Gilbert, Xavier, and Paul Strebel. 1988. "Developing Competitive Advantage." In J. B. Quinn, H. Mintzberg and R. M. James, eds., *The Strategy Process: Concepts, Contexts and Cases.* Englewood Cliffs, N.J.: Prentice-Hall.

Gilley, Otis W., Gordon V. Karels, and Robert P. Leone. 1986. "Uncertainty, Experience and the 'Winner's Curse' in OCS Lease Bidding." *Management Science,* Vol. 32, No. 6 (June): 673–682.

Hackman, J. Richard. 1986. "The Psychology of Self-Management in Organizations." In M. S. Pallack and R. O. Perloff, eds., *Psychology and Work: Productivity, Change, and Employment.* Washington, D.C.: American Psychological Association.

Hannan, Michael T., and John Freeman. 1989. *Organizational Ecology.* Cambridge, Mass.: Harvard University Press.

Haspeslagh, Philippe. 1982. "Portfolio Planning: Uses and Limits." *Harvard Business Review,* Vol. 60, No. 1 (January–February): 58–73.

Hayes, Robert H., and David Garvin. 1982. "Managing as if Tomorrow Mattered." *Harvard Business Review,* Vol. 60, No. 3 (May–June): 71–79.

Henderson, Rebecca. 1990. "Successful Japanese Giants: A Major Challenge to Existing Theories of Firm Capability." Mimeo, Massachusetts Institute of Technology (December).

Hendricks, Kenneth, and Robert H. Porter. 1988. "An Empirical Study of an Auction with Asymmetric Information." *American Economic Review,* Vol. 78, No. 5 (December): 865–883.

Henry, Claude. 1974. "Investment Decisions under Uncertainty: The 'Irreversibility Effect.'" *American Economic Review,* Vol. 64, No. 6 (December): 1006–1012.

Herrnstein, Richard J., and Drazen Prelec. 1991. "Melioration: A Theory of Distributed Choice." Working Paper No. 89-030, Harvard Business School.

Howard, Ronald A. 1966. "Decision Analysis: Applied Decision Theory." In D. B. Hertz and J. Melese, eds., *Proceedings of the Fourth International Conference on Operational Research.* New York: Wiley-Interscience.

———. 1988. "Decision Analysis: Practice and Promise." *Management Science,* Vol. 10, No. 6 (June): 679–695.

Hunt, Michael S. 1972. "Competition in the Major Home Appliance Industry, 1960–1970." Unpublished Ph.D. dissertation, Harvard University.

Janis, Irving L., and Leon Mann. 1977. *Decision Making: A Psychological Analysis of Conflict, Choice, and Commitment.* New York: Free Press.

Jones, Robert A., and Joseph M. Ostroy. 1984. "Flexibility and Uncertainty." *Review of Economic Studies,* Vol. 51, No. 1 (January): 13–32.

Judd, Kenneth L. 1985. "Credible Spatial Preemption." *RAND Journal of Economics,* Vol. 16, No. 2 (Summer): 153–166.

———. 1990. "Cournot versus Bertrand: A Dynamic Resolution." Mimeo, Northwestern University (March).

Kahnemann, Daniel, and Dan Lovallo. 1990. "Timid Decisions and Bold Forecasts: A Cognitive Perspective on Risk Taking." Mimeo, University of California at Berkeley (September).

Kahneman, Daniel, and Amos Tversky. 1979. "Prospect Theory: An Analysis of Decision Under Risk." *Econometrica,* Vol. 47, No. 2 (March): 263–291.

Kester, W. Carl. 1984. "Today's Options for Tomorrow's Growth." *Harvard Business Review,* Vol. 62, No. 2 (March–April): 153–160.

Klammer, Thomas P., and Michael C. Walker. 1984. "The Continuing Increase in the Use of Sophisticated Capital Budgeting Techniques." *California Management Review,* Vol. 27, No. 1 (Fall): 137–148.

Klein, Burton H. 1984. *Prices, Wages and Business Cycles.* New York: Pergamon.

Knight, Frank H. 1921. *Risk, Uncertainty, and Profit.* Boston: Houghton Mifflin.

Kreps, David M., and A. Michael Spence. 1984. "Modeling the Role of History in Industrial Organization and Competition." In G. Feiwel, ed., *Contemporary Issues in Modern Microeconomics.* London: Macmillan.

Lancaster, Kelvin. 1971. *Consumer Demand.* New York: Columbia University Press.

Levine, Michael E. 1987. "Airline Competition in Deregulated Markets: Theory, Firm Strategy, and Public Policy." *Yale Journal on Regulation,* Vol. 4, No. 2 (Spring): 393–494.

Libby, Robert, and Peter C. Fishburn. 1977. "Behavioral Models of Risk Taking in Business Decisions: A Survey and Evaluation." *Journal of Accounting Research,* Vol. 15, No. 2 (Autumn): 272–292.

Lichtenstein, Sarah, Baruch Fischoff, and Lawrence D. Phillips. 1977. "Calibration of Probabilities: The State of the Art." In H. Jungermann and G. deZeeuw, eds., *Decision Making and Change in Human Affairs.* Amsterdam: D. Reidel.

Loomis, Carol J. 1979. "How I.T.T. Got Lost in a Big Bad Forest." *Fortune,* December 17: 42–55.

Magaziner, Ira C., and Mark Patinkin. 1989. "Cold Competition: GE Wages the Refrigerator War." *Harvard Business Review,* Vol. 67, No. 2 (March–April): 114–124.

Mansfield, Edwin. 1981. "How Economists See R&D." *Harvard Business Review,* Vol. 59, No. 6 (November–December): 98–106.

McKenzie, Lionel. 1960. "Matrices with Dominant Diagonals and Economic Theory." In K. J. Arrow, S. Karlin, and P. Suppes, eds., *Mathematical Methods in the Social Sciences.* Stanford: Stanford University Press.

Merrow, Edward W., Kenneth E. Phillips, and Christopher W. Myers. 1981. *Understanding Cost Growth and Performance Shortfalls in Pioneer Process Plants.* Santa Monica: RAND Corporation.

Milgrom, Paul, and John Roberts. 1986. "Relying on the Information of Interested Parties." *RAND Journal of Economics,* Vol. 17, No. 1 (Spring): 18–32.

———. 1990. "The Economics of Modern Manufacturing: Technology, Strategy, and Organization." *American Economic Review,* Vol. 80, No. 3 (June): 511–527.

Miller, Danny. 1990. *The Icarus Paradox.* New York: Harper Collins.

Miller, Danny, and Peter H. Friesen. 1984. *Organizations: A Quantum View.* Englewood Cliffs, N.J.: Prentice-Hall.

Mintzberg, Henry. 1990. "Strategy Formation: Ten Schools of Thought." In J. Fredrickson, ed., *Perspectives on Strategic Management.* New York: Ballinger.

Neumann, John von, and Oskar Morgenstern. 1944. *The Theory of Games and Economic Behavior.* Princeton: Princeton University Press.

Newhouse, John. 1982. *The Sporty Game.* New York: Alfred A. Knopf.

Pascale, Richard T. 1984. "Perspective on Strategy: The Real Story Behind Honda's Success." *California Management Review,* Vol. 26, No. 3 (Spring): 47–72.

———. 1990. *Managing on the Edge.* New York: Simon and Schuster.

Pohlman, Randolph A., Emmanuel S. Santiago, and F. Lynn Markel. 1988. "Cash Flow Estimation Practices of Large Firms." *Financial Management,* Vol. 17, No. 2 (Summer): 71–79.

Porter, Michael E. 1980. *Competitive Strategy.* New York: Free Press.

———. 1985. *Competitive Advantage.* New York: Free Press.

———. 1986. "The NFL vs. the USFL." Intercollegiate Case Clearinghouse No. 9-386-168.

———. 1987. "From Competitive Advantage to Corporate Strategy." *Harvard Business Review,* Vol. 65, No. 3 (May–June): 43–59.

———. 1990. *The Competitive Advantage of Nations.* New York: Free Press.

Prelec, Drazen. 1991. "Values and Principles: Some Limitations on Traditional Economic Analysis." In A. Etzioni and P. Lawrence, eds., *Perspectives on Socio-Economics.* Armonk, N.Y.: M. E. Sharpe.

Prigogine, Ilya, and Isabelle Stengers. 1984. *Order Out of Chaos.* New York: Bantam.

Reinhardt, Uwe E. 1973. "Break-Even Analysis of Lockheed's TriStar: An Application of Financial Theory." *Journal of Finance,* Vol. 28, No. 4 (September): 821–838.

Rumelt, Richard P. 1987. "Theory, Strategy, and Entrepreneurship." In D. J. Teece, ed., *The Competitive Challenge.* Cambridge, Mass.: Ballinger.

———. 1989. "How Much Does Industry Matter?" Mimeo, Anderson Graduate School of Management, University of California at Los Angeles (July).

Sah, Raaj Kumar, and Joseph E. Stiglitz. 1986. "The Architecture of Economic Systems: Hierarchies and Polyarchies." *American Economic Review,* Vol. 76, No. 4 (September): 716–727.

Sahlman, William A. 1991. "The Structure and Governance of Venture Capital Organizations." *Journal of Financial Economics* (forthcoming).

Sakiya, Tetsuo. 1982. *Honda Motor: The Men, the Management, the Machines.* Tokyo: Kodansha International.

Samuelson, Paul A. 1976. *Economics.* New York: McGraw-Hill.

Savage, Leonard J. 1971. "Elicitation of Personal Probabilities and Expectations." *Journal of the American Statistical Association,* Vol. 66, No. 336 (June): 783–801.

Schall, Lawrence C., Gary L. Sundem, and William R. Geijsbeek, Jr. 1978. "Survey and Analysis of Capital Budgeting Methods." *Journal of Finance,* Vol. 33, No. 1 (March): 281–287.

Schlaifer, Robert G. 1959. *Probability and Statistics for Business Decisions.* New York: McGraw-Hill.

Schoemaker, Paul J. 1990. "Strategy, Complexity and Economic Rent." *Management Science,* Vol. 36, No. 10 (October): 1178–1192.

———. 1991. "The Scenario Approach to Strategic Management." Mimeo, Graduate School of Business, University of Chicago (January).

Schweiger, David M., and William R. Sandberg. 1989. "The Utilization of Individual Capabilities in Group Approaches to Strategic Decision-making." *Strategic Management Journal,* Vol. 10, No. 1 (January–February): 31–43.

Shaked, Avner, and John Sutton. 1987. "Product Differentiation and Industrial Structure." *Journal of Industrial Economics,* Vol. 36, No. 2 (December): 131–146.

Shapiro, Carl. 1989. "The Theory of Business Strategy." *RAND Journal of Economics,* Vol. 20, No. 1 (Spring): 125–137.

Skinner, Wickham. 1981. "Big Hat, No Cattle: Managing Human Resources." *Harvard Business Review,* Vol. 59, No. 5 (September–October): 106–114.

Smith, Douglas K., and Robert C. Alexander. 1988. *Fumbling the Future.* New York: William Morrow.

Staw, Barry M. 1981. "The Escalation of Commitment to a Course of Action." *Academy of Management Review,* Vol. 6, No. 4 (October): 577–587.

Stevenson, Howard H., Daniel F. Muzyka, and Jeffrey A. Timmons. 1987.

"Venture Capital in Transition: A Monte-Carlo Simulation of Changes in Investment Patterns." *Journal of Business Venturing,* Vol. 2, No. 2 (Spring): 103–121.

Sutton, John. 1991. *Sunk Costs and Market Structure.* Cambridge, Mass.: MIT Press.

Tichy, Noel, and Ram Charan. 1989. "Speed, Simplicity, Self-Confidence." *Harvard Business Review,* Vol. 67, No. 5 (September–October): 112–120.

Tushman, Michael L., William H. Newman, and Elaine Romanelli. 1987. "Convergence and Upheaval: Managing the Unsteady Pace of Organizational Evolution." *California Management Review,* Vol. 29, No. 1 (Fall): 1–16.

Tversky, Amos, and Daniel Kahneman. 1981. "The Framing of Decisions and the Psychology of Choice." *Science,* Vol. 211, No. 4481 (January): 453–458.

Vancil, Richard F. 1981. "General Electric Company: Background Note on Management Systems." Intercollegiate Case Clearinghouse No. 9-181-111.

Waterman, Robert H., Jr. 1987. *The Renewal Factor.* New York: Bantam.

Weitzman, Martin L. 1983. "Contestable Markets: An Uprising in the Theory of Industry Structure: Comment." *American Economic Review,* Vol. 73, No. 3 (June): 486–487.

Wells, John R. 1982. "Owens-Corning Fiberglas: Commercial Roofing Division (A)." Intercollegiate Case Clearinghouse No. 1-383-040.

Whitten, Ira T. 1979. "Brand Performance in the Cigarette Industry and the Advantage to Early Entry, 1913–1974." Report to the Federal Trade Commission, Washington, D.C. (June).

Williams, Jeffrey R. 1988. "A Perspective on Our Expanding Markets." Mimeo, Carnegie-Mellon University (January).

Williamson, Oliver E. 1975. *Markets and Hierarchies.* New York: Free Press.

———. 1985. *The Economic Institutions of Capitalism.* New York: Free Press.

———. 1990. "Strategizing, Economizing, and Economic Organization." Mimeo, University of California at Berkeley (October).

Wright, J. Patrick. 1979. *On a Clear Day You Can See General Motors.* Grosse Pointe, Mich.: Wright Enterprises.

Zajac, Edward J., and Max H. Bazerman. 1991. "Blind Spots in Industry and Competitor Analysis." *Academy of Management Review,* Vol. 16, No. 1 (January): 37–56.

Zysman, Simon J. 1973. "Top Management and Decentralized Investment Planning in Diversified Firms: A Comparative Study." Unpublished DBA dissertation, Graduate School of Business Administration, Harvard University.

Index